shaped by the story

DISCOVER THE ART OF BIBLE STORYING

MICHAEL NOVELLI

DEDICATION

To my brother Mark

who has walked with me through the entire storying journey over the years.

Your continual encouragement and input

have shaped this book and my life in immeasurable ways.

First edition published 2008. Second edition published 2013.

Cover and interior design: Mark Novelli, IMAGO

ISBN 978-1-4514-6942-4

17 16 15 14 13 1 2 3 4 5 6 7

contents

introduction

Now more than ever, I'm fascinated by the Bible.

Since I was a teenager, I've learned that the Bible is full of wisdom; I've searched its pages for principles to live by. But I was always looking to unearth the meaning behind the meaning—the pattern or the nugget that was applicable to my life. And I spent years studying and teaching the Bible this way.

Over the last several years, however, I've come to view the Bible in a different—and, I believe, more holistic—way. I now view the Bible as a *story*.

I love how stories have the power to take us on a journey. They show us new places and introduce us to new people. They draw us in, and we become a part of their adventures. And the best stories give us a glimpse of ourselves—they show us who we are and who we could be.

The Bible is like this. It stretches from the beginning of time, across our lives, and into the future. It tells of a great and faithful creator who reveals the most beautiful way to live: in rhythms of love, peace, and restoration.

This story has incredible meaning for our lives. Its intent is for us to find ourselves in it and to be *shaped by the story*.

WHY I WROTE THIS BOOK

After ten years in youth ministry, I felt as though I'd tried everything to help my students connect with the Bible. Then, when a missionary named John Witte taught me the art of Bible storying, I realized it was more than just a new way to teach. It was a complete shift in how I could help students with their spiritual formation. It changed everything about the way I now look at my faith and ministry. Bible storying made such a big impact on me that I've spent the last decade helping others discover this amazing way of experiencing the Bible.

My hope is that you will experiment with Bible storying. I have created resources with Sparkhouse, but this is not a sales pitch to buy my products. I genuinely want you to see that Bible storying is more than a curriculum, but a way of encountering God through the Bible.

WHO THIS BOOK IS FOR

The wealth of my ministry experience is in youth ministry—twenty years and counting! I love high school students, and hope to continue to serve them for years to come. My approach to Bible storying does come from a youth ministry context but has expanded to ministry with people of all ages. I touch on some of those experiences in Chapter 5. I believe if you lead a group of any kind, you will find this book and Bible storying beneficial.

CLARIFICATIONS AND EXPECTATIONS

Throughout this book I'll use the words *narrative* and *story* interchangeably to describe a sequence of events that includes characters, dialogue, context, and plot. The Bible contains hundreds of stories. I'll also use the term "the Bible's story" to describe the entire collective narrative found in the Bible.

I've discovered that the best way to let the Bible shape us is to experience it as story—to hear it, read it, and embrace it as a narrative. I regard the Bible as a living story—a sacred account that's illuminated and brought to life by the Spirit of God. This book is about how we might allow the Bible to form our lives. That may sound simple but, as you probably know, life formation is a complex journey.

In order to take this journey with me, you must be open to:

› Interacting with the Bible in new ways

› Letting go of your expert status and becoming a colearner

› Expecting parts of the Bible's story to be illuminated to each person

› Having fun, laughing, and enjoying learning

› Focusing on spiritual formation rather than information acquisition

What you shouldn't expect to get from this book:

› A formula for ministry success

› A trendy postmodern or "story" curriculum

› A foolproof method without possibility for failure and human error

› A process that leads to one conclusion or application from Scripture

› The only effective way to teach or learn the Bible

This book is more of a starting point than a comprehensive guide. It marks where I am, and what I've learned over the past ten years in my journey with storying. I hope you'll benefit from the examples of my experiences of leading storying. I encourage you to step out, explore, let go, and try something new.

Bible storying is something better experienced than explained. At the end of each chapter there are also questions to think about and discuss. For further resources, training, and ideas about storying, go to **www.wearesparkhouse.org**.

WHAT'S NEW IN THIS EDITION

Shaped by the Story was first published in 2008. This new edition has been revised with over 30 percent new content. Here is some of what I have updated:

> Methods for adapting Bible storying for varied contexts and ages

> New testimonials from people using this approach with children, youth, and adults

> Additional tools to create your own Bible storying narratives and dialogue questions

> Details about the proven learning theories guiding this approach

Since this book first went to press, I have continued to improve my approach and learn more about Bible storying. I have tweaked and added to this method based on research and experience in order to make it more effective. I hope the improvements open up pathways to make the Bible more accessible to people of all ages, and, more importantly, to create space for God's Spirit to work in and shape our lives.

PART **ONE**

my storying journey

CHAPTER ONE

PROGRAMS & PEP RALLIES

My first memory of the Bible is from Mrs. Mary's preschool class in the Methodist church basement in our small town. Mrs. Mary had short black hair and wore pointy thick-rimmed glasses. She beamed with kindness. Hugs and back-rubs abounded and she called us all "sweetie." With a patient rhythm she moved about our class, kneeling down to our level to look in our eyes, encourage us, and give a gentle nudge if we needed redirecting.

My twin brother Mark and I enjoyed almost every minute of learning and playing in Mrs. Mary's sunshine class. Midmorning, after juice and graham crackers, Mrs. Mary corralled us to sit quietly on an old frayed area rug. She opened a big trunk full of all kinds of hats, shirts, and props for us to bring the day's Bible story to life. My brother and I called them "plays," and they were quite memorable.

The most vivid story I remember us enacting was Jesus healing people with leprosy. Mark and I (along with a few other students) were selected to play sick people in the story, while my friend Jeff was picked to play Jesus. I wondered why Jeff often got to play Jesus, and thought it must be because he was the tallest in the class. When I asked him, Jeff said, "I get to play Jesus because I live down the street." Hum. Jeff must have had a special connection because he could walk to class. Maybe he came early and rehearsed his role as Jesus!

Mrs. Mary asked us to put "leprosy spots" (made from purple clay) on our arms. Some of the kids were excited, but my brother and I wanted no part of this. In fact, we were terrified, fearing these spots would somehow make us sick and never come off. So when Mrs. Mary began narrating story, we both hid under a table, well out of the teacher's reach. After some negotiating, we came out from under the table. We brokered a deal that promised that no "sores" would be applied to our arms, but we still had to let Jesus heal us. A fair trade-off, I thought.

As a child, Bible stories seemed scary to me—storms, wars, sickness, spitting in people's eyes, blood, demons. No thanks. We preferred Mom's stories about talking animals and magical forests over Mrs. Mary's Bible stories any day.

While I was growing up, the Bible seemed like an ancient history book to me, full of weird stories that I had no interest in reading. I remember spending one long Sunday afternoon watching *Family Classics* presentation of *The Ten Commandments*. I was probably seven years old, and even then I could tell Charlton Heston's beard was a fake. And when he broke the two big "stone" tablets on the ground, I could see they were obviously Styrofoam. How lame! I thought. "Come on, Mom. Can we turn on *Battlestar Galactica*?"

I did like the part when Moses parted the sea and got electrocuted on the mountain. Oh, wait a minute, the lightning actually missed him. He still seemed pretty dumb for carrying around a big stick on a mountain in a lightning storm.

> As a child, Bible stories seemed scary to me— storms, wars, sickness, spitting in people's eyes, blood, demons. No thanks. We preferred Mom's stories about talking animals and magical forests over Mrs. Mary's Bible stories any day.

My journey of faith was a path left mostly unexplored until I reached high school. Some friends invited my brother and me to a church youth group during my sophomore year. I had a growing interest in spiritual things, but little understanding. It was the first time I had ever attended a church service outside of a wedding or funeral, and the first time I had ever read the Bible. Youth group was a place where I quickly built friendships (and was a good place to meet girls).

The youth leader from the church, Dan, told me that in order to grow spiritually I needed to have "devotions." This seemed odd to me: "Why do I need to read the Bible on my own if we're going to read it together?" Still, I began flipping around in the Bible aimlessly, like throwing darts at a board. After sifting through some of the books, I often landed in the books of Proverbs and James. These seemed the best places to find a quotation that would help me be a better person and live virtuously. At the time, I thought that religion was just about living morally.

One night after youth group, Dan pulled me aside and started firing questions at me about why I came to church and why I read the Bible. I'd just begun dating a girl from the youth group, and Dan said, "We don't let Christians date non-Christians." I wasn't sure what he was talking about. Was he talking about the girls I was friends with at school? I never thought of myself as a "non-Christian," and I'd never considered that there was an "us and them" thing going on. (Even now, I don't think this way of thinking is helpful.)

I told Dan, "I'm new to church. But I think people are at different levels with all of this." He immediately showed me several verses about sin and separation from God, asking me if I understood that I was a sinner. "We all mess up," I replied.

Then he showed me a verse about how I needed to confess with my mouth and believe in my heart that Jesus is Lord. He asked me, "Who do you believe Jesus is?"

"God's Son?"

"Do you really believe that in your heart?" he interrupted.

I paused; he stared at me. "Yeah," I gulped. I was sweating, and I felt as though he was cross-examining me. I wanted Dan to like me. He was a good guy, fun to hang out with, and so genuine with us in the youth group. I was afraid I'd get kicked out if I doubted or had any questions. Yet I wasn't sure what it meant for Jesus to be "Lord."

Then Dan said, "You don't have to have all the answers to your questions; you have to have faith. If you really believe that, then say it out loud."

"Say what?" I asked.

"Jesus is Lord," he said.

I parroted, "(gulp) Jesus is Lord?"

Then he prayed for me. When we opened our eyes, he asked me, "Do you feel different?"

"I'm not sure, what should I be feeling?" I answered.

"Well, you're changed now," Dan replied.

We talked some more. Dan told me the Bible is really about Jesus, and he encouraged me to read the Gospel of John. I went home and began reading that night. I was riveted by this story, and I read the Gospel all the way through in one sitting. Jesus was such a fascinating person and said and did such powerful things. In the next few weeks, I read and reread John. Then I read the other Gospels. This was good stuff! It was one of the best stories I'd ever read—one I wanted others to know too.

I told Dan what I'd been reading, and I asked him how I could help other people know about this story. He taught me to draw a bridge diagram with Bible verses and simple steps to explain how to get to heaven. I asked, "Why not just have them read the story about Jesus?" One of the other youth leaders told me, "People need more than the story; they need to know how to be saved."

This answer didn't satisfy me, but I wasn't sure why. It got me wondering why we needed the other parts of the Bible. We rarely talked about them in church, and I didn't see how they had much to do with Jesus. But my church insisted that the whole Bible is God's words. I was confused. The Old Testament was sometimes described in church as a "law book" that shows people how they can't live up to God's standards. That sounded depressing—why would I want to read that?

Thankfully, my doubts and questions didn't prevent me from wanting to learn more. The story of Jesus was so powerful that I couldn't stop thinking about it. The love that Jesus showed for people seemed so different—it made my heart leap and stirred me toward wanting to help others know about this remarkable person.

So after high school, I attended a small Bible college to study theology and ministry as a vocation.

One of my pivotal classes was hermeneutics—how to interpret the Bible. This course taught us how to "exegete" passages of Scripture using a set of historical-critical skills. I was told that if I used these skills correctly—in tandem with the study of a passage in its original language—then I could arrive at the "true meaning" of the text. It was emphasized to me that there are "many applications to Scripture, but only one interpretation."

> This was the ministry one-two punch—historical-critical exegesis followed by expository preaching.

Then came a course in homiletics—how to prepare and preach a sermon. I was primarily taught the expository preaching method—a systematic way to teach a continuous segment of Scripture. This approach taught me to select a passage of Scripture, study it carefully, and try to uncover the key points—usually three or four of them. Then I was to support each one of these points with related stories and Bible verses. To conclude, I was to tell my audience how to live out these concepts in their daily lives. This was the ministry one-two punch—historical-critical exegesis followed by expository preaching.

During college I began leading a middle school ministry called Discovery. At the time, I was only twenty years old and new to Christianity. Those are years of ministry that I wish I could do over. Despite my mistakes, students from that youth ministry still tell me it was a positive and important group in their lives.

At first I tried expository preaching with these middle schoolers, but I gave up on it pretty quickly. They didn't seem interested in learning from the Bible–they looked like they were going to fall asleep. Meanwhile, down the hall we could hear pounding music, cheers, and laughter from the burgeoning high school ministry. The rock-star high school pastor didn't teach with exposition, and his topical style of teaching seemed to have his students in a frenzy for Jesus. So I started modeling my approach to teaching after his.

I would find a topic that seemed current or relevant and develop a message around it with a biblical perspective. I made it as entertaining as I could using props and humor. But as time went on, I began to feel as though our youth groups were just pep rallies for Jesus. Even though this was never articulated, our focus seemed to be to charge students toward a state of continual emotional high that would catapult them to live for God.

I felt out of place there. I could not be the hype-guy. It just isn't the way I am wired. I desired to help my students explore a faith that went deeper than emotion and positive stimulus.

I spent the next few years volunteering in a megachurch's high school group. I had experience in running events and in creative arts, so I helped brainstorm and put together some of the weekly programs for the youth ministry. Excellence, cultural relevance, applicability, and authenticity were high values for our team. It was a fun group to serve with—they loved students and really desired to help them connect with God.

Our programs were mostly topical, focusing on Christian living. I felt as though the content had depth to it, but it rarely focused on learning from the Bible. Instead, it emphasized ideas that we felt were supported by the Bible. So we spent lots of time trying to determine what topics we should teach, usually picking the ideas we thought were the most relevant to students.

As I continued to serve this large group of students, I began to notice some interesting things. The big stage, professional lights and sound, and well-crafted programs and messages all created a different kind of youth ministry than I'd ever seen before. It seemed as though the majority of the students came to observe or evaluate rather than participate. They were audience members instead of members of a community.

Our creative team invested countless hours and creativity to put together programs that were engaging and interactive, but it was difficult to tell if what we planned made a difference. Week after week, droves of students sat back in our theater-style chairs with their arms folded and offered little reaction.

Ironically, I also noticed that some of the students had a deep desire to be on the stage. Those teenagers in the band, drama, dance team, and especially those who helped with the teaching were revered as insiders—celebrities. I became concerned that we were feeding a culture that was already enamored with entertainment.

I sensed that significant changes were needed in our ministry. But how? How could we help students connect with the Bible if our primary means of communicating with them was through a presentation on a stage?

QUESTIONS FOR REFLECTION AND DISCUSSION

> *What parts of this story do you relate to?*

> *What Bible stories have most captivated you?*

> *What have you been taught about why we read the Hebrew (Old) Testament?*

> *How do you read the Bible? In what ways have you changed the way you read it?*

> *What kind of teaching do you best connect with?*

> *How do you teach the Bible? How do you determine what you will teach?*

A TRUE STORY ABOUT STORYING

About four years ago I was at a crossroads. I had been in working with youth for about 16 years at this point and was starting to really question my impact on their lives. As I talked with friends also working with students, they were seeing some of the same things. It seemed like much of what I ended up teaching turned into behavior modification lessons, "If you want to follow Jesus, you have to do this, but don't do that".

I struggled with this since the motivation for students seemed to land with pleasing parents or myself, not following God. That is when I was introduced to the work Michael Novelli was doing. After reaching out to him and having him come and share chronological Bible storying with our youth and children's ministry staff, I decided to make a change in our approach to teaching the scriptures. Now as a youth group we are on our third time through the scriptures from Genesis to Revelation discovering the story for God.

Even when we are not following the overarching story of Scripture, we have taken a chronological storying approach. We have taken large sections of time and looked at only the Judges of Israel and also a semester looking at only the life of Jesus. The greatest part of this is that students have the background knowledge to create context for what we are dialoguing over. We have amazing discussion about the scriptures and students are sharing profound truths they are learning.

This has a great learner–centered focus, and I have the chance to talk to students about their relationship with God. They are making decisions based on what the Bible teaches and really wrestling with what God desires for their lives. We have even taken this year as a church and are going through the entire story together chronologically. Adults are making connections that they have never seen before, and the story is coming alive for them. Together as a church we are experiencing the story of God and discovering how to live that out together in our life context.

—**STEVE CORNELIUS**, YOUTH PASTOR FROM POPLAR, WISCONSIN

CHAPTER TWO

EXPOSITION & STAND-UP COMEDY

How do I help make relationships central to ministry?
How do I help students take ownership of their spiritual growth?
What form does learning need to take to really connect?

These were the questions swirling in my mind from serving two years with programming at a megachurch. Right after that experience, I took a position as a high school pastor at a large congregation in the western suburbs of Chicago. The main thrust of this church's energy and resources was focused on Sunday services—of which an expository sermon was the centerpiece. These weren't elements that attracted me to that church; it was the opportunity to lead a paid staff team for the first time and the freedom to shape a ministry. My hope was to focus the ministry on relationships, Bible learning, and spiritual growth.

The middle school pastor and I developed a plan to base our teaching topics on theology. We designed a teaching cycle for sixth through twelfth grades, covering thirty-two core Bible principles and virtues. Our plan seemed comprehensive and intentional. But was it ever complicated. It was like looking at the periodic table of elements. I remember trying to explain this plan to parents and other staff members, and they all responded with a glazed-over look. Their eyes said, "Good luck trying to pull that off!"

Despite the underlying complexity of our plan, my style of teaching was more straightforward and laid-back. I strove to be practical and conversational, full of questions and stories. It wasn't long before church leadership strongly encouraged me to stick to expository teaching to stay in step with the church's philosophy.

Preparing expository messages was tough for me because I'm not very conceptual, but I'm analytical. So when I'd try to examine, dissect, and draw out main points from a passage, I'd enter into a temporary paralysis: What if I'm missing the "right" points? Where can I find the perfect illustration to go with this? It was common for me to anguish over each point of every message, trying to perfect it. I would be entombed in research for days, trying to take in and distill as much knowledge on the subject of my message as humanly possible. And all the while, I'd be thinking in the back of my mind: Why do I go through this every week?

Part of this was my neurosis—but not all of it. A portion of my discomfort with this approach came from feeling as though my ideas about the Bible, rather than the actual Bible, were center stage. I found that expository preaching often centers more on the main points that I choose to draw from the text, rather than the text itself. That means I could fit the Bible into my presentation, controlling it by the text I picked and how I supported each of my main points. I'd tell students what the passage said and then, as specifically as I could, share how they should live it out.

What was even scarier was how I found myself following some bad examples of expository teaching, saying things such as, "What Paul is saying here" or "What Jesus is telling us is" as if I'd uncovered what Paul and Jesus were *really* trying to say. Yikes.

I'm sure there are thousands of people more gifted at expository preaching than I. Perhaps there are many more who are also truer to the process. But my experience, after trying to teach this way for more than ten years, is that this method is basically just an informed speech about Scripture—one person's educated opinion (usually borrowed from other educated opinions). Where this often led me was to a feeling that preaching was much more about my performance than my content. Students only seemed to focus on how engaging, entertaining, compelling I might be. All the while my students sat back with arms folded, (possibly unconsciously) evaluating me. This made me wonder, why should this be about *me* and my skills? Why am I doing all the work of learning and connecting with God? Shouldn't this be about us—together— seeking God?

One thing that really bugged me as I taught was that it seemed as though my supporting illustrations were the only things the students remembered. I'd pour myself into a message, passionately share it, and the only thing students would say afterward was, "That story about when your friend crapped his pants at Six Flags was hilarious!"

Thanks, dude. Did you hear anything else?

I still have former students send me messages about some of the funny stories I told them years ago. I enjoyed making students laugh, but it was never my primary goal. As time went on, I began to resent the idea that I was just a stand-up comedian to them. It seemed as though the students filtered out all the other (more important) stuff I was saying and locked onto the humor. I guess if I were just sitting in an audience with a hundred others I'd do the same thing. That's what an audience is conditioned to do—sit back and pick out what seems useful or entertaining. Audiences are conditioned to be consumers.

> That's what an audience is conditioned to do—sit back and pick out what seems useful or entertaining. Audiences are conditioned to be consumers.

I also feared that we were giving our students a brand of Christianity that was too simple and too shallow—irrelevant to the complexities of the life they would soon face in college. I was certain our teaching method was contributing to this; it felt as though all we were doing was digesting the Bible for our students and regurgitating it back to them in bite-size pieces, like a bird to its young.

I was determined to help students connect with the Bible without always having to be the intermediary. I told our volunteers, "If the Bible is a living book that can change lives, then let's help students learn from it directly." We began meeting in house groups where a few small groups met under one roof with adult guidance. We moved these house groups to our primary meeting night each week and provided caring adults to reach out to every student who came.

One of our adult volunteers told me about an inductive Bible study she was leading with girls from our youth group. She expressed how the approach she was using really helped get her girls into the Bible. I investigated this method further, and I liked it too. This method seemed to direct people deeper into the text to search for the intended context and meaning. It was also simple enough that most anyone could do it. I was on board!

I spent a few months developing a training guide for our students. Then we spent a month training a core group of our students to lead these Bible studies with their peers. Adult coaches sat in on these small group sessions to make sure students focused on studying the Bible and kept on track theologically.

Two months into this process, we had some meetings to evaluate how this method was working in our groups. I got positive feedback from adult leaders who loved that we were focusing on teaching the Bible. But only a handful of the students were excited about how it was going. The majority of the students complained it was like school—too much reading, thinking, and underlining—and their group was bored by it. A few students said it didn't apply to their lives—they wanted to talk about dating and real-life stuff. (I'm convinced there are a few students in every youth group who'd like us to teach about dating every week.)

As I asked for feedback in this meeting, students got into disagreements with each other. I felt like a referee—and I admit, I kind of enjoyed it. At least they were passionate about learning! A few students drove the conversation and were adamant about our continuing to study the Bible this way. One student said, "The Bible is like our textbook for life. We need to study it like we would at school." I mostly agreed with him. My initial reaction to our group was, "Suck it up. Being a Christian takes work. If you want to grow, then you have to study the Bible; it will pay off later." Then I added, "I'm not running a YMCA here." I regularly gave this reply when students complained about the group not being fun enough. (I'm pretty sure they hated my saying this.)

But the core question wouldn't go away: why were most of my students struggling with this method? At first I thought it was a lack of initiative created from being conditioned to be consumers and not participants. But after many discussions, I discovered that the vast majority of my students wanted to be in the group and learn more about God. It made me wonder: Is the Bible too cryptic for them to relate to on their own? Do we really have to tell them what it says?

I observed each of our small groups in an attempt to uncover the real issues. And as I visited these groups, I noticed some interesting patterns.

First, a good majority of the students struggled with reading and comprehension. Many couldn't define simple words and struggled with reading aloud. This was especially surprising coming from upper-middle-class families within highly rated school systems. Yet high literacy is essential to most Bible-study methods, so this was a big problem.

Second, my students had very little Bible knowledge and background. How could this be? The vast majority of these students had grown up in our church. It didn't seem to matter what book of the Bible we picked to study: they didn't understand how it fit into the larger story. With only a few exceptions, students struggled to understand simple Bible terms such as Jews, gentiles, the law, idols, and so on. Even more of a concern was the fact that the majority of the students didn't believe it was important to understand the background of the passage.

Which led to my third observation: discussions moved quickly to tangents and personal opinions. Little time was given to discover the author's intent. Most of what was shared were observations that students and adults heard in church and students' observations about the Bible. Then they'd tack on any meaning they wanted, even if it had nothing to do with the passage. Context didn't seem important.

I was battling uphill against an ingrained approach to the Bible held by both our students and adults that I call *proverbializing*—treating the Bible as if it is just a collection of proverbs. I saw our groups skimming over the Bible like a self-help book, looking for bite-sized moral quips and handy life lessons. It seemed we'd learned to sift through the Bible in search of a nugget of truth to extract, then ascribe our own meaning in order to apply it to our lives.

Essentially, the Bible became just a conversation starter in our groups. I worried that this was my fault. Maybe I didn't train them to follow the process correctly. But I soon discovered that the process wasn't the main issue; it was my group's perspective of and relationship with the Bible.

I asked Dean, a student leader in our youth group, for his honest feedback. He said, "I like to read—but this is different. I read the sections over and over—it feels like I'm trying to decode something. I'm really trying, but I feel like I just don't get it. Maybe this isn't the way that I learn." "Well, how do you learn?" I replied. He answered, "I am not sure."

> Embarrassingly, I never really thought much about what are best approaches and environments for learning.

I was troubled by this conversation. What did he mean this isn't the way he learns? How else do you learn from a book than studying it? Why did Dean love to read fiction books, but reading the Bible was a struggle?

I had no idea what to do. It seemed as though we were missing our students. I sensed a disconnect between the Bible and students' lives. I realized that I was giving students only one way to approach the Bible—one based solely on critical analysis. This seemed to cause us to dissect the Bible, extracting only single ideas from it. We needed an approach to the Bible that would engage us both critically and creatively, analytically and emotionally.

My conversation with Dean also caused me to consider how my students learned. For more than a decade of youth ministry I had invested a lot of energy in trying to improve how I teach. I worked hard at connecting, at being engaging and poignant. Embarrassingly, I never really thought much about what the best approaches and environments for learning are. I started conversations with my wife, who is an educator, about the ways that different people learn. These conversations and research would alter the course of how I have been doing ministry ever since.

But changes were coming in our youth ministry. The church leadership was becoming concerned that my ministry was too focused on small groups and not on a large program. They wanted someone who would lead the youth ministry primarily through preaching and upfront presence. I didn't fit this model they were moving toward, and I felt my opportunity for influence was shrinking fast, so I resigned.

Then I really hit rock bottom. I started sniffing glue, and I lived in a dumpster. (Not really. I just wanted to see if you were still reading.)

QUESTIONS FOR REFLECTION AND DISCUSSION

> *What parts of this chapter do you relate to? How?*

> *What challenges have you faced in helping others engage with the Bible?*

> *How does your group typically interact with the Bible?*

> *Why do you think people might struggle with a literate, study-focused approach to learning the Bible?*

> *How have you found ways to help others take ownership of their spiritual growth?*

> *What kinds of Bible studies have you been a part of? In what ways were they helpful and not so helpful in studying the Bible?*

A TRUE STORY ABOUT STORYING

I've rarely—if ever—seen students connect with and respond to Scripture the way they have through storying. Not only that, but also my own passion and interest in God's Story have grown and deepened in ways that I never could've imagined.

Having led the storying process, it's been one of the absolute thrills of my life and work in ministry to watch students become enthralled with the story of God, finding themselves completely caught up in (and a part of) the characters, patterns, and themes of the Bible.

I, like many others, had gotten to a point where I not only struggled each week to engage students in deep, meaningful dialogue about God and his ways, but I also found myself struggling daily to engage with God in my own life. It would be an overstatement to call storying the cure-all for both problems—but it sure feels close.

Having been a part of the storying process, both as a participant and a leader, I can truly say I'm unwilling to retreat to former, more familiar modes of learning and teaching the Bible. It's not that I find no merit in them. It's not that I won't try anything else. But I won't go back. I'm not sure I can go back.

Seeing (and teaching) the Bible as the story of God and God's people throughout history (with today's church being the latest chapter of that story) has changed my life and ministry in unalterable ways.

—**KELLY DOLAN**, VOLUNTEER FROM ARLINGTON HEIGHTS, IL

CHAPTER THREE

SPEAKING THE SAME LANGUAGE

After leaving the big church, my wife and I attended a small church in the same area. I volunteered to work with the youth group, and I soon found myself serving as the part-time youth director. I wasn't looking for a job, but this seemed to be a good fit for the church and for us.

For the first three or four months, I just observed the group and tried to build relationships with the students and volunteers. About twelve students attended the group each week; most were Christian-schooled or homeschooled. I'm not exactly sure how this played into the social dynamics of the group, but they showed little interest in each other. They'd often find the walls of the room and stay there. Needless to say, there was a lack of enthusiasm and energy in the group.

Many of the students' parents forced them to attend. After observing the group for a couple of months, I began leading their programs. We immediately made some changes as we tried to build a sense of community and momentum. For instance, we began meeting in a home to create more of a family environment (this also helped us to include more volunteers with small children). We also played games to get students talking and having fun.

More students from the church began attending, but I think this was at the prompting of their parents, who wanted to give me a chance. One of the students asked me, "So how long are you going to be here? We've had a different youth pastor every year for the past four years. I just want to know how long you plan on staying."

I wasn't sure how to answer this. I said, "I hope to be here a long time." He rolled his eyes a bit at my reply, and I began to understand why these students didn't engage: they hadn't had consistent leadership or relationships. This gave me a bit more compassion for these students and a little more patience with their apathy.

It was obvious to me that most of these students had a lot of prior exposure to Christian teaching and practices, and this familiarity caused some of them to see God as being commonplace and small. More than any other group I'd worked with, there was an underlying attitude that they knew it all.

I tried to connect with them using my best messages and activities from the large church I just left, but they seemed indifferent. During one of my teachings, a student raised her hand and asked, "This is good. But can I work on my homework now? I have a test tomorrow." Ugh. I felt defeated and a little desperate, not knowing how to reach this unique group of students.

About the same time I began working at this new church, a friend invited my brother, Mark, and me to a chronological Bible storying training session in our area. I had never heard of this approach and was not even sure why I was there. As we entered the room, about twenty-five people sat around a big table. We soon discovered most all of them were training to serve in overseas missions. John Witte, a missionary to Africa, led the workshop. He was a tall, thin, Southern man in his late forties, with salt-and-pepper, crew cut hair. He began the training by telling us how for more than ten years he'd been teaching Bible stories to indigenous people in Africa, helping them to form an "oral Bible." I thought to myself, what is an oral Bible?

Many of the people John encountered had never even seen a written word, yet they learned deep truths about God through hearing, discussing, and retelling Bible stories. The people of these tribes would sing songs and create chants about the stories, and then they'd share the stories with other villages. John had seen how chronological Bible storying (CBS) was transforming lives among the tribes he worked with. He shared story after amazing story of how this approach to teaching was affecting people in Africa. (Read more of John's story in appendix H.)

John found that leaving his Jeep behind, walking to different tribes, and living among the people was the most effective way of connecting with them. By walking to the tribes instead of driving,

John communicated his desire for equality, respect, humility, and patience to care for the people with whom he was sharing Bible stories.

One of the stories John shared with us described an informal case study his denomination carried out comparing the Bible knowledge of oral learners to that of their literate seminary students in Kenya. Through this study, researchers discovered that the tribal people, who learned just from oral stories, showed as much—or more—depth of theology as those who learned from a seminary's systematic literary methods.

I was fascinated by John's experiences, but restless as I thought about my know-it-all students, and how this didn't seem to apply to them. They'd heard Bible stories over and over from the time they were little.

But after sharing the impact of storying in Africa, John led us through a Bible storying experience something akin to what he did with tribal people. He told more than thirty Bible stories, mostly from memory (this was something he called fast-tracking the Bible). These weren't loosely paraphrased stories but accurate narratives with key dialogue. I was amazed at how much of the Bible John had memorized, and I was even more amazed at how captivated we all were by these stories.

I have a hard time staying focused in many situations. (Maybe it has something to do with being raised in front of a television.) But these stories grabbed my attention and kept my interest like no sermon had ever done. It felt similar to reading a novel in which the story unfurls in your mind right before you and all of the pieces fit together at the end.

In between most of the stories, John led us in a time of retelling and dialogue. By asking pointed questions, he helped us discover connections and details about the characters that we'd never seen before. Theology was surfacing, and I was learning new things in a new way from stories I'd read dozens of times before and had thoroughly studied in college. I had never seen a teaching approach like this that was deeply experiential and theological at the same time.

This was the first time I'd ever seen how the Bible's stories interconnect as one great metanarrative, with themes of covenant, redemption, restoration, and kingdom woven through the entire story. I was taught to look at only parts of the scriptures, examining collections of true statements to study in small segments. Rarely did I hear the Bible told as story—and never like this. This experience completely changed the way I teach and look at the Bible.

> I was taught to look at only parts of the scriptures, examining collections of true statements to study in small segments. Rarely did I hear the Bible told as story—and never like this.

After the training, I had dinner with John. As we talked, I got to hear more of his stories from the mission field and about his family. At one point in the conversation, John asked me directly, "You seem really excited about this method. How do you plan to use it?"

I stumbled over my words, finally saying, "I'm not sure. I'd like to try this with my youth group, but I'm concerned because I'm sure they've heard these stories a million times."

John replied, "You have too, right? How did you respond?" (He was doing that Jedi mind thing he's so good at—helping me find my own answers.)

"Yeah. You're right. I need to help them come to the stories in a new way."

Then John said, "God's story is living. If we really trust that, then we'll listen to it and learn from it our whole lives. Not too many people are trying storying here in North America. You need to think bigger than your church. People need this here, especially teenagers. You're the right one to figure this out." John was convinced the story approach would work well in American culture, which is already captivated by stories.

I didn't know how to respond. I was scared. I thought, I can barely memorize my phone number—how can I do this? How can I help people in other churches when I'm not sure I can help the students in my youth group?

I asked, "Can you show me some of your stories to help me get started?"

John said, "Sure, but I'll have to write them down. I've been meaning to do that anyway."

I thought, what a freak—he doesn't even have them written down. Oh yeah . . . this is going to be real easy.

I nervously asked, "How important is it that I memorize the stories?"

John said, "I think it's the best way to do it. It's critical that the stories become a part of who you are . . . and that takes time. Be patient. You'll figure it out. God will help you."

I knew he was right. I'm impatient, and I'd switched to logistics mode already. Even though I was intimidated by the task of figuring this out, I felt something stirring in me. I needed to explore this further.

I still wasn't sure how my youth group with their heard-it-all attitudes would respond to the Bible stories, but I was willing to try it. Soon after the training, I put together a night where we told the stories of the lost coin, the lost sheep, and the lost son. I didn't teach about them or give background information. I worked with two of my adult volunteers to help them tell the stories as stories, instead of just reading them.

Before we began, I told the students to listen to the stories as though they'd never heard them before—and really concentrate. Afterward, we broke up into our small groups for discussion. I let volunteers lead the discussions using questions I'd written based on the Bible storying method I learned from John. The questions guided us toward observation, asking: What did you notice for the first time in the story? What did you learn about God? What did you learn about humans? And so on.

As soon as the discussion started, I noticed a different tone in our group than I'd seen before. They seemed interested in sharing and listening to each other. That night we achieved one of the most engaging Bible discussions that I'd ever had with students. They actually wanted to talk about the Bible.

It seemed as though telling the scripture as a story was a key that unlocked something for us—as if we were now all speaking the same language. For the first time, students wanted to keep talking about the stories until after it was time to go home. Parents were waiting at the door.

After the students left that evening, I had our regular feedback meeting with the adult volunteers. My wife and the other leaders shared similar responses from their students: "Our group wouldn't stop talking and giving input. This is the first time that's happened." "This really got them thinking about the story; usually they just talk about their own problems."

> It seemed as though telling the scripture as a story was a key that unlocked something for us— as if we were now all speaking the same language.

This was in the spring, and I wanted to figure out a way to experiment with this method of teaching throughout the upcoming school year. I immediately started working on narratives. I hoped that the stories I was stitching together from the scriptures would be a bridge that got my students excited about learning from the Bible, and would lead them to read it for themselves.

I started with twelve stories, but felt compelled to expand this into a set of twenty-one stories from Genesis to Acts. I used a list of stories that John Witte gave me as a guide in choosing which stories to tell. The goal was to put together a set of stories that would paint a picture of God's restorative plan—"a redemptive arc." I aimed to remain true to the biblical texts, preserving key events and dialogue. I did my best not to embellish with my own additions or elaborations. I wasn't trying to "modernize" the stories; I just wanted to tell them chronologically and accurately.

I spent months comparing English translations as I stitched together the narratives. I smoothed over language and simplified parts that seemed overly repetitive. I studied key passages in the original Hebrew and Greek to try to ensure that I was representing the text well. It was a worthy investment that initially took me more than 1,200 hours over a sixteen-month period. By the fall I was close to halfway finished with my first attempt at stitching together narratives. I was far enough along to begin telling these stories with my group. The experiment would soon begin.

QUESTIONS FOR REFLECTION AND DISCUSSION

› *Which parts of this chapter did you relate to your own story?*

› *How do people in your group view the Bible?*

› *Why do you believe people connect with stories?*

› *How have you incorporated storytelling in your ministry?*

A TRUE STORY ABOUT STORYING

Storying is actually one of my favorite things to do. I get really excited when God speaks to me through other people. I love the sense of mission that comes when we talk in a community about God's story and what God is like. The characters in the Bible have become more human and earthy since we started going through the stories. There are actually, literally, three dimensions to God's story and to all its characters. All the stories in the Bible happened on the same planet we're on right now. And each little piece (such as the story of Joseph or the story of God's covenant with Abraham) doesn't stand on its own. It's part of a greater tale. God is so big—and God's story can be known only through a saga. And no single picture describes God, either. The only way humans can attempt to illustrate God is through a story that spans the whole history of the earth.

Through the stories, I'm realizing that God actually wants me and the life I'm living to become a part of restoring his garden of Eden dream for the world. I don't know if there's anything more beautiful than a God who dreams of peace and wholeness to come to all creation.

For me, the story of the Bible reveals God's dream for the world. Knowing the story of God's interaction with human beings allows me to find my place in the activity of God's kingdom. As his church, we can begin working toward realizing God's dream for all people. Knowing the story helps me know how to continue that story. Seeing what God has been working to accomplish in human history allows me to take my place in this plan of restoration.

By realizing that God's dream is for humanity to be united and connected, sharing our lives and resources with one another, I can give myself to making that happen in my life. The kingdom of God won't be a destination only in the future; it can be a present reality that grows through the healing of our broken souls as we come to find life in our creator.

Through the story I'm realizing that inner transformation propels God's kingdom. As we see God's story come to life and as we begin to see our world with God's eyes, we can be changed on the inside and then bring change to the people and places we find around us. God's story shows us God's heart for all creation, and we see the wholeness and love God has for human beings.

And as humans who are being made whole, we can work toward God's dream that the world will be more beautiful and that we'll restore it, connecting our hearts with God's to bring shalom—peace and wholeness—to the whole world.

—**NATALIE POTTS**, HIGH SCHOOL STUDENT IN EAST SAINT PAUL, MINNESOTA

CHAPTER FOUR

THE STORYING EXPERIMENT

At the beginning of the next school year, I began a nine-month process of telling, retelling, and discussing Bible stories with my youth group. I was a little surprised at first when the students didn't know how to react to them (since they seemed so excited by the initial trial). As we went through the first two stories, they asked questions such as, "So when are you going to teach us?" "Why aren't we studying the Bible?" and "What does this have to do with everyday life?" And I'd usually respond, "Trust me. Be patient with this; we're going to try something new. We're not getting rid of our Bibles. In fact, I think this will get you more interested in reading them." I felt as though we were going through a detox program together—trying to strip off all the layers of expectations regarding how we're supposed to come to the Bible. It required a lot of patience, grace, and consistent yet gentle reminders of why we were doing what we were doing.

The first few weeks were challenging. I could see the "we've heard this story a million times" look in their eyes. But when we got about three or four stories into the process, the students began to see how the stories are interrelated. They shared connections between the creation story, the disruption story, and Cain and Abel.

But one of my students seemed frustrated. She asked, "Why don't you tell us how to apply this story?" I responded, "I am so glad you asked that. I am not going to tell you how to apply these stories to your life. You are going to tell me! You see, God inhabits these stories. If you are really listening and using your imagination to put yourself in these stories, God will stir something in your heart and mind. Each of you will see something different—something meaningful. When that happens—and it will—you need to share it with the group . . . because you are becoming the teachers. Every week, I come expected to learn from you as God speaks through you."

The group was completely silent. They looked at me like I was crazy. They knew that I was not giving up! I was on a mission to help them realize that God was at work already in each of them. This was a commitment to affirm their creativity, insight, and ability to connect with the divine. From that moment they began to believe that I really wanted to hear their observations; some also began to believe that God was sparking connections in their minds to the Bible story and their own lives. We were building a different culture of learning.

Students' excitement about the stories was building. I could tell because their level of engagement was so much higher; they wanted to retell the stories and offer their observations—without being asked. They were becoming more and more engaged. Things weren't perfect, though. There were still distractions, and some students disengaged at times, but overall, we were becoming a different group—a community forming around the Bible's story.

> **This was a commitment to affirm their creativity, insight, and ability to connect with the divine.**

Each week, after our mealtime, we'd review the previous stories we'd covered. I tried to make this creative and fun, involving them in art, drama, music, and so on. The reenactments of the stories were often hilarious—and surprisingly accurate. We used symbols for each story to help us connect with something visual. Reviewing the stories also helped any new people get up to speed on what we'd already covered.

After the review, I'd briefly share a metaphor to help us prepare to listen to the story. I called it getting in "imaginative listening" mode. One of these metaphors went something like this:

> Listening to these Bible stories is like being an eyewitness to an important event. We can use our imaginations to be there—to see the story in our minds like we're there when it's happening. What's interesting is that each of you sees the story from a different place or vantage point. You each notice different things about it. So what you see—even if

it's simple—is important to help us each get a better picture of what this story means to us. Your unique perspective matters. The things you write, draw, and share make a difference even if you think they are small. Each of you helps us, as a group, to see and understand more about God.

Let's take a moment and get ready for imaginative listening. Set aside any distractions or tiredness, and really try to put yourself in this story. The further we go in this story, the more detailed it gets, so it takes more concentration to let your imagination kick in. If it helps you, close your eyes during the story or you can sketch or write down things that stand out to you. Are you ready? Take a moment in silence right now to take a deep breath, slow down, and clear your mind. Whisper a prayer asking God to show you something meaningful in this story.

> I realized early in the process that my job was to be more of a guide than an instructor, leading our group on the journey into the Bible's story. We'd learn and explore together, and I'd help frame our experiences and keep us on the path. Most of the time I felt as though I was learning as much as my students were.

These introductions to the story helped our group get into the right frame of mind. I used (and continue to use) some variation of this every week because the storying process is very repetitive. I knew some of my students who are used to constant change through media might lose focus. I had to be mindful of this tendency and continually coach them to be attentive.

I realized early in the process that my job was to be more of a guide than an instructor, leading our group on the journey into the Bible's story. We'd learn and explore together, and I'd help frame our experiences and keep us on the path. Most of the time I felt as though I was learning as much as my students were.

The storytelling time was never more than ten minutes long, and I really worked at trying to bring the story to life with my voice, rather than just reading it. With my first group we kept it low-tech. I never used music, visuals, or video. (Sometimes we'd light a candle to symbolize the beginning of the imaginative listening mode.) This isn't to say those tools can't help, but I was concerned that in such a small group they'd become more of a distraction than a vehicle toward building imagination and listening.

We'd sit in a circle in one of our students' living rooms, and after the storytelling we'd do a quick group retelling to recount the events of the story. I led this time by asking questions such as, "What happened first in the story? What happened after that?" Sometimes we'd do a fun group retelling of the story, using all kinds of learning methods like drawing, acting, readings, tag-team tellings, etc. (I have since replaced this retelling with a reflection and capturing time, which I will explain in detail later in chapter 11.)

As we reviewed and retold the stories, something very interesting began to happen—something I call "communal correcting." The group began to work together and help each other remember key details. When someone missed something or said something inaccurate, the group would correct him or her— usually in a gentle way. This was better than my stepping in as "the expert" and setting things straight.

> ## The Storying process I first followed with my group:
>
> › **REWIND**
>   previous stories
>
> › **PREPARE**
>   for the story
>
> › **IMAGINE**
>   the story
>
> › **REPLAY**
>   the story*
>
> › **CONNECT**
>   with our story
>
> * [Later changed to CAPTURE what you notice]

Following the retelling, we'd engage in a dialogue about the story. I'd usually begin this time by setting up some ground rules: Everyone is expected to participate, your observations matter, this isn't about offering answers but rather observations, and no jumping ahead to future stories—only connect the current story to ones we've already covered in the chronology.

The first questions I'd ask were "wondering" types of questions, such as, "What stood out to you from this story?" "What did you picture in your mind as the story was being told?" and "What does this story make you wonder about?" This really helped disarm the students, and it allowed them to use their imaginations. When students asked questions about the story out of wonder (for instance, "Who was Cain afraid would attack him if he and his family were the first humans?"), I wouldn't give my opinion or an expert's answer; I'd just affirm them, saying, "That's a great question. I wonder about that, too" or "Would someone be willing to research that a bit this week and share what you learn the next time we meet?"

This took my students some getting used to because they expected me, the Bible teacher, to give them all the answers. But by allowing this kind of wondering and tension, we provided space for us to explore the realities of the stories in our imaginations and bring them into the realm of relatability, giving us a sense that there is always more to explore within the story.

After our dialogue time, we broke into small groups—usually one boys' group and two girls' groups. Chris, my intern, led the guys' group most of the time, and I observed. We sometimes called these "my story groups," as the focus was on sharing ways we saw our own stories connecting with God's story and with each other. We never told the students how to apply the stories, but we did ask some pointed questions, such as, "How does this story challenge or encourage you to live?" and "How is this story our story? How is it your story?" These times were filled with honesty and amazing insights from our students.

One of the new guys in our group began sharing his story. He was a small, quiet sophomore, and we really didn't know much about him. Still, he opened up about his life, and he shared how he'd brought his mom to our church and it had changed their lives. Then he said something I'll never forget: "I'm learning more than ever before. I saw that I really wasn't a believer. The stories pulled me back in." He broke down and began crying, which led to a long, awkward silence. Then, spontaneously, the other guys got up and embraced him, and many of them started crying, too. These were guys who wouldn't even say hello to each other just months earlier, and now they were embracing in a giant group hug. Wow! The other volunteers and I sat there in awe.

Each week I gave out cards with the Scripture for that week's story. Without my prompting, students were coming back the next week with observations and questions after reading more about the story. The story sparked a desire to learn more and to actually read the Bible. A few students told me they read more about the stories everyday. And one student sarcastically asked me in front of the rest of the group, "Why didn't you tell us Noah got drunk and naked at the end of the story?" Even though this wasn't a funny part of the story, our whole group burst out laughing.

We took a month off over Christmas break. When we resumed in January, we did a review of all the stories from the fall. At the beginning of our time together, I handed out cards with our symbols for each story written on them, and I asked the students to pair up and put the stories in order. We'd gone through about ten stories so far, and I assumed they'd struggle to remember some of them. The students worked together with only a few disagreements, and they had all of the stories mostly in the right order. I think I had to switch only two people around. So far, so good.

Then I asked the students to tell us what they knew about the stories on their cards. So beginning at creation, we went down the line, and some students told the stories word for word. Caesar and I looked at each other in amazement. Jacob and Esau, the Exodus, the Tabernacle—these are stories with lots of details, and the students were retelling most of them. I was so encouraged to see them excited about God's story, I was in tears.

One student asked, "What's wrong, Mike?"

"Don't you see?" I said. "God's Story is capturing each of you. It's becoming a part of your stories."

One student shared, "I feel like these stories are talking about me." A few of the other students laughed when he said this. I interrupted them, "I think you are right. Can you tell me more about that?"

He replied, "These stories are giving me a picture of how I should and shouldn't live. I can relate to the struggles of the Israelites . . . it makes me see how much I need God."

"Yeah, this is pretty cool," another student replied.

It wasn't about memorization; it was about students being excited about how the Bible could change their lives.

Momentum was building now, and students began inviting their friends to our group. One of the girls said, "I wasn't too sure about this idea at first, and I didn't really want to invite my friends to come and hear old Bible stories. Really, I thought it was for kids. But once we got into it, it was way better than I expected. And my friends really wanted to come and learn." This was a girl who seemed disengaged most of the time, but she became a magnet for bringing friends to our group.

I also noticed that a volunteer's wife was now coming every week. She was so involved in the kids' ministry and music ministry at the church that I knew she didn't really have time to come to youth group. But she said to me, "I've taught these Bible stories for years, but this is new and different. I want to come every week to find out what's going to happen next in the story and to see the 'light bulbs' go on."

"Well," I teased, "you can read ahead."

We saw these students become transformed by the Bible's story. Do you know how I could tell change was happening? The questions, observations, and connections they were making went deeper and deeper each week.

One of the guys shared with our small group, "I find myself telling these stories to some of my friends at school—and some of them don't know about Jesus at all. It's also inspiring me to write songs about God." For several weeks he came back with stories about how his friends were interested and asking questions about the stories at the lunch table.

During her first visit, one girl shared, "I've never heard these stories before; they're really interesting." A few weeks later, she opened up to the girls' small group, telling them, "Tonight, I realized that the stories you're telling are going a different direction than my own life. How can my life be a part of what you're doing?" The girls and adult leaders encouraged her and prayed for her and drew her into their community.

Around Easter we held a Messianic Seder with our students. (A Seder is a symbolic Jewish meal that's held during the annual Passover celebration in remembrance of how God rescued the Hebrews from their slavery in Egypt.) This was our second year of hosting a Messianic Seder for students, but this one was different. The experience seemed much richer because we were already immersed in the story.

We prepared an elaborate Jewish-style meal for the students, complete with many traditional Passover items. The word Seder means "order," so we followed a Haggadah—which means "explaining"—a booklet I developed filled with prayers, readings, and points of interaction. We began the Seder with the exodus story and concluded with the Last Supper story.

This celebration came alive right in front of us, giving powerful new meaning to the symbols, imagery, and rituals of the exodus. It also helped us connect the stories of Abraham's covenant and the new covenant in Jesus, giving us a deeper understanding of Jesus as the Messiah. All of us who took part in this Seder were deeply moved by it, and it continued to be one of the most powerful moments I've ever experienced in youth ministry.

"Aren't we supposed to be God's blessing to others like Abraham was?" one student asked. "Well, my brother and I have a couple of ideas about this." This student initiated opportunities for our group to regularly serve meals to the homeless, and he began to rally students in his school to join in this movement. He did all of this because he saw himself as a continuation of the Story—to be God's blessing to the world.

A few weeks later we came to the story of Jesus's death and resurrection. I was concerned that students were too familiar with this story. But I was wrong. The story gave us another entry point to reflect on the sacrifice of Jesus. Students related the details of this story back to the tabernacle, the Passover, and the words of the prophets. There were nonstop connections taking place, adding even more meaning and depth to our times together. One student said, "It's amazing how at the end you realize how all of the stories connect—they all point to Jesus."

Instead of going to our small groups, the students initiated an impromptu prayer time. For thirty minutes they prayed out loud, giving thanks, crying, and expressing their hearts to God.

Two weeks later we had a celebration to finish the school year. We grilled food and had a lot of fun playing games outside. The students' parents came that night, too. The highlight for me was a sharing time during which the students wrote on cards and then shared how the Bible's Story had shaped their lives over the past school year.

Here are just a few of the responses from these students:

> The stories challenged me to look beneath the surface and search for more about God's character. I learned something new from every single story.

> I saw these stories in a new light. I want to read them over and over again!

> I [now] see that the Bible isn't boring but full of amazing info. And stories that can impact my life.

> I couldn't stop thinking about the stories. Some of the questions were so difficult that they made me want to go and search for the answers.

> The stories changed my whole perspective on my faith. They made me want to live for God because God is amazing—and those stories prove it.

> The stories and discussion really challenged the way I viewed the Bible and the perspective I've had about Christianity. It really helped me dig deep and actually

understand the story. I'm now challenged to live [my life while remaining] open to whatever Jesus calls [me to do].

I realized that God is the author of my life . . . and is writing my story that I'm so excited to discover! We must keep the story going and ask God where we belong in the story.

I was deeply moved by what my students shared. It honestly surprised me. I expected that along the way my students would gain a better understanding of the Bible. I hoped they would experience God and want to read more from the Bible. But I did not anticipate how this experience would begin to shape my students theology and identities right in front of me. They were looking for God—in the Bible and in each other. The language they used was deeper than what I was used to hearing from students—it reached beyond the surface of behavior to the core of their own identities.

> **The language they used was deeper than what I was used to hearing from students—it reached beyond the surface of behavior to the core of their own identities.**

Toward the end of our youth group time, one of the parents pulled me aside. "I need to talk to you," she said. I was a bit concerned, as she was a protective homeschooling mom who was also very vocal. I worried I'd done something wrong. Then she said, "My son has been learning about the Bible in homeschool his entire life. But this year has been amazing. He's learned more from these stories about God than from anywhere else."

I replied, "Thank you, that's so kind of you to say. I'm not sure that's really true, though. I believe that all of your investment in his learning now has a context. These stories have helped your son develop a mental timeline so he can see and understand all that you've taught him from a broader perspective."

This experience transformed not only my group, but it also changed me. I was shaped by the story. It ignited a passion in me to want to connect more with God through the scriptures, and to help provide this approach as a pathway for other groups to connect with the Bible in a new way.

QUESTIONS FOR REFLECTION AND DISCUSSION

> *Which parts of this chapter did you relate to your own story?*

> *What are the similarities and differences between storying and your current teaching methods?*

> *In order to be effective, what do you believe Bible storying requires from the leader? From the participant?*

> *How do you think your group might respond to Bible storying? What challenges do you believe you'd face? How might it help them to learn?*

A TRUE STORY ABOUT STORYING

I've been in youth ministry for eleven years, and I'm enjoying it now more than ever. Most of this has to do with my experience with storying. Over the last couple of years, storying has helped me to discover new and meaningful ways to be a spiritual guide for my students and young adults. As we've gone through the stories, I'm encouraged by the depth and meaning that my students share from their lives. Storying provides us with opportunities to share observations and struggles and to reveal what we're grasping from the Bible. By listening to my students share, I've gained tremendous insight into what's going on in their minds and hearts.

Storying has helped me feel free and excited to teach in a new way. It seemed as though teaching in more traditional ways depended so much on what I brought—the right points, the right prop, the right joke, the right video—in order for students to learn. Now, through storying, I feel as though we're partners. I'm continually learning from my group as we move through these sacred stories. Each week a number of the students come back to our group—unprompted—with something they've researched, helping us dig deeper into a part of the story they had questions about or didn't understand.

Storying has helped me really believe that God will speak to and through my students if they'll work to enter the story. This is something I'd lost hope in, but now I continue to see God reveal to us new things about who he is and who we are. God is surprising us with new things we've never thought of before, and God continues to open up our perspectives on how big, mysterious, and beautiful he really is.

As I drove home from the house group last night, I pictured in my mind Anna, Todd, Ricky, Alex, and many of the other students who were there. I was moved by the experience we'd shared together as a diverse group—students and adults who are black, Latino, or white; some are rich, some are middle class, and some are poor; some are attending college, struggling in high school, or dropping out of high school.

For the first time in more than a decade of ministry, I've found a way to connect people with the complex, deep truths found in the Bible. God has reminded me again that wherever two or more of us are together, God is present, lovingly speaking and revealing himself to us.

—**SETH McCOY**, YOUTH WORKER IN SAINT PAUL, MINNESOTA

CHAPTER FIVE

ECHOING THE STORY

After experiencing Bible storying with my first youth group, I was filled with excitement and questions. Why did this seemingly simple approach connect with my students in such deep ways? I wondered if it was just a one-time, unique experience with this group, or if it would resonate with other groups in similar ways. I had many friends in youth ministry, and I couldn't contain my enthusiasm about Bible storying, so I told them about what happened with my group.

GROWING MOVEMENT

My brother Mark and my best friend, Jeff, were the first to jump in and try storying with their youth groups. I cleaned up my set of twenty-one Bible narratives and dialogue questions for them to use. They both led large youth ministries, and asked me to come and lead a workshop just for their youth leaders to prepare them for this unique approach. I had so much fun sharing my ideas and walking alongside these groups as they began this experiment. There were, however, growing pains with trying to implement this with hundreds of students and dozens of adult leaders. The biggest challenges seemed to be getting adult leaders to believe that they did not (should not) have to provide answers and applications.

> The biggest challenges seemed to be getting adult leaders to believe that they did not (should not) have to provide answers and applications.

At the end of their nine-month experiments, I was encouraged to hear that this approach was also transformative for their groups. Here are some of the responses they received:

> I wasn't too sure about this idea at first and I didn't really want to invite my friends to come and hear old Bible stories

. . . but once we got into it, it was way better than I
expected and my friends really wanted to come and learn.
—LINDSEY, STUDENT

I had no idea that I would learn so much from stories I have
heard all my life.
—STEPH, STUDENT

This was the best interaction I have had with my group of
girls about the Bible since I started working with students. –
SUE, YOUTH VOLUNTEER

I was amazed at the level of engagement and excitement
towards the stories that the students and leaders showed
over the course of the year. They not only remembered
the stories, but were excited to dig deeper into the Bible
for themselves to learn even more about them.
—MARK, GROUP LEADER

I realized that Bible storying was more than just a new way to teach.
It was a complete shift in how we could help students with their
spiritual formation. It was about helping students become learners
and observers of the Bible and life.

Workshops

I never set out to start a ministry. I was a youth pastor just trying
to help my students connect with God and the Bible. But within
months of helping Mark and Jeff implement Bible storying, youth
workers began contacting me wanting to learn more about it. By
word of mouth, I started getting invitations to lead workshops. I
discovered that I really enjoyed leading workshops and continued
to hear remarkable things about how storying was sparking interest
in the Bible with other youth groups.

To try and better serve others, I formed a ministry called Echo the
Story. With help, I created a website to share resources and story sets.
That's when things got really busy. I am not sure how people heard
about the website, but dozens of people each day started logging
on and contacting me. Over the course of three years, thousands
of people signed up to get more information about Bible storying—
from over fifty countries! I started leading workshops and retreats

in Bible storying all over the North America. Over the past six years, I've had the privilege of leading over one hundred workshops in "The Art of Bible Storying." Honestly, I am amazed and humbled by the responses I continue to receive. I attribute this not as my own personal accomplishment, but that I am fortunate to be a part of a larger movement of God reinvigorating a narrative approach to experiencing the Bible.

More Stories

Throughout this book are segments called True Stories about Storying. These are stories from youth workers who have been encouraged by how Bible storying has connected with their group. My hope with this is not to try to sell this method to you, but rather for you to read first hand and be encouraged and inspired along with me.

STORYING WITH MY CURRENT YOUTH MINISTRY

The year after leading my first Bible storying group I moved to a different city, and I began serving with a ministry reaching out to urban youth. For two years, I invested in relationships with the most impoverished and hurting teens I'd ever met. Most of my role was behind the scenes, so I did not have many opportunities to shape the teaching. I did, however help them to try Bible storying over a four-week stretch. It was really interesting to see how storying reached across culture, socioeconomic status, and race to captivate our students. I continued to encourage youth workers in urban contexts in the Chicago area through workshops and relationships, networking with them through North Park University.

While working with urban teens in our community, I also began to serve with a youth group at a local church a few blocks from my house. I became so connected with this group of teens that I eventually phased out my work with the urban ministry. I continue to serve with this church youth ministry as a volunteer leader, helping to give shape to our weekly teaching.

Our youth group is made up of students who've grown up in our church and are rooted in our church culture. There is a healthy sense of intergenerational connectedness. Time after time I have heard graduating seniors remark how they feel supported and accepted by our church family. But this connection does not necessarily equate to a firm articulation or ownership of faith. About one third of our students say they are agnostic, and another third seem to be deeply searching and questioning their faith. This has created some unique challenges for us.

For the first several years of working with my group it was strongly recommended by church leadership that we use the denominational publishers youth curriculum. I, and the other youth leaders, struggled along for years trying to adapt this curriculum. This curriculum was narrative-based, and they'd developed strong components for children. But the youth curriculum did not connect with our students. It assumed a level of adherence to faith and a desire from students to want to worship through singing and crafts. Our students had so many questions about Christianity that they simply would not participate in an authentic way.

> We could not start trying to experience the Bible and dialogue about it without first exploring why it is meaningful to our lives right now. There had to be some consensus that exploring the Bible has value, or storying simply would not work.

Recently, I was given the opportunity to experiment with Bible storying, using a set of twelve core stories I'd been developing. This set of stories gives a quick Bible overview from Creation to the Church. Unlike the first time I used Bible storying, I went into this experience with high expectations about the results. Surely my students would be captivated by this approach as so many groups have been over the last several years, right? Well . . . we hit a lot of snags.

We tried to jump right into the first lesson about Creation, but a few of the students didn't want to study the Bible—they did not find value in it. And they were vocal about it. Essentially they expressed that the Bible seemed like an antiquated story used by people to try and justify small-minded views about science, prejudice, and violence. Wow. Did I mention we had (and still have) some challenges?

So we had to back up. We could not start trying to experience the Bible and dialogue about it without first exploring why it is meaningful to our lives right now. There had to be some consensus that exploring the Bible has value, or storying simply would not work. So we spent a few weeks just talking about how we might come to the Bible in a meaningful way.

One of the weeks, I discovered that my students were not sure what I meant by the words *story* and *narrative* (I give a definition in chapter 6). More than just understanding what a story is, they wanted to know what I meant by the word *story*. Did I mean *story* like *The Hunger Games* (fictional) or *Zero Dark Thirty* (fictionalized history), or a documentary film (actual events)?

I realized that it is important for me to be clear about how we should interact with the Bible as story. This is more difficult than it sounds. I am still thinking about and working on a description.

I began by asking my group, "What are some ways in which people see the Bible?" I wrote down their responses on a big piece of paper: wisdom, to-do list, fantasy, rules, ancient history, rulebook and so on.

We grouped the responses in these categories:

FANTASY	SACRED STORY	INSTRUCTION MANUAL	HISTORY BOOK
Fables that contain some wise teachings	Ancient accounts of people's experiences with and beliefs about God	Life principles, wisdom, and moral truths	A literal record of events describing God's laws for and rescue of humans

I said, "There's another way in between these views of the Bible. We can look at the Bible as a sacred story." Then I added to the chart "Sacred story: Ancient accounts of people's experiences with and beliefs about God."

I continued, "Most of the Bible—about 75 percent—is actually narrative, meaning it was written in the form of a story. The ancient Israelites and early Christians who gave us the stories in the Bible weren't trying to report events like modern journalists or historians. Instead, they were telling stories of their experiences and what they believed about God's activity in the world. Many of the stories they told were passed down to generation after generation.

A sacred story is a different kind of story, combining literal and poetic descriptions of reality to reveal deep truths. The ancients were not worried about getting every detail exactly right; what they wanted to ensure was that their beliefs and perspectives where preserved. This is an in-between way of looking at the Bible because it conveys that the Bible is both reality and metaphor mixed together."

This explanation surfaced questions, such as:

"So which parts are metaphor and which parts are facts?"

"Is it all a made-up story?"

"How can we trust the Bible if we don't know what really happened?"

"I thought the Bible is God's words (Word)? Shouldn't it be 100 percent accurate if God wrote it?"

My answer to these questions went something like this: "For a long time I was told that the Bible was dictated by God word-for-word to people who recorded everything that God spoke to them. But as I have read the Bible more and more and grown in my understanding, I see this a little differently now.

Most of the Bible is a collection of stories about a special group of people's encounters with God. God inspired them in such a real way that they couldn't help but share these encounters with their families and community. And they described these encounters in the best ways they could, according to their ancient understanding of how God, science, and the world works. For generations, these stories got passed down by word of mouth.

I think most all of these stories are (historical) true events at their core, but they are history remembered and retold. Not every detail was translated or conveyed exactly as it happened, but the essence is intact. The purpose of the stories in the Bible are not to provide us with some detailed historical record; they are stories that are intentionally embedded with beliefs to be passed down to each generation.

> The purpose of the stories in the Bible are not to provide us with some detailed historical record, they are stories that are intentionally embedded with beliefs to be passed down to each generation.

Ancient Near Eastern cultures didn't think like us—like left-brained scientists, focusing in on empirical thought and evidence and accuracy. They thought in a more fluid, poetic, and big-picture way. It was far messier. They didn't worry about contradictions—in fact, they welcomed them. Sometimes before they would tell a story they would say things like, 'This was, and this was not.' or 'I am not sure if this story happened exactly this way, but I know it is true.' Kind of mind-bending. So the stories did not have to be 100 percent verifiably true events to be truth. I believe that through our imaginations and reflection on these stories, God helps reveal to us the truths embedded in them. These stories are sacred because they are a unique revelation of God to us. They give us a glimpse of who God is and how God wants to work through us in the world."

In order for us to explore the Bible as a sacred story, we must ask different kinds of questions. Questions like:

1. **What do you notice?** We will be entering the Bible's stories with our imaginations—like eyewitnesses who will then share what we have seen and sensed. This helps us to move beyond the two-dimensional world of an ancient story in a book to an experience that had multi-dimensions and depth of meaning.

2. **Why would they (the Israelites and First Christians) tell this story?** These stories that arose out of a remarkable,

beautiful, strange and mysterious culture. These are their sacred stories—stories they risked their lives to preserve and pass down to us. So we should come to them with reverence and awe.

3. **What does this story say about us? What does it say about me?** Embedded in these stories are deep truths that can provide meaning for us in this moment. The wealth of meaning is inexhaustible, as the stories are uniquely multivalent.

The idea of the Bible as sacred story seemed to help provide a usable lens even for our skeptical students. So we restarted Bible storying. And it did start out better. A few weeks later, following the Exodus story, a student asked, "So if these stories are supposed to show us what God is like, does that mean God is a murderer who commits genocide? There is too much violence and contradiction in the Bible. I can't believe in a god that is like that."

I cobbled together a response that went something like this, "In many ancient cultures, people thought that most everything that happened in life was a result of favor or punishment from a deity. If the crops died, it must be punishment from (a) god. The Israelites thought like this, too. They told this story through their human understanding. I think there are parts that they thought were God's words and actions that were not—like God calling for genocide.

> More than just a cloud or fire or wind, God came and lived with humans in human form. This was God recalibrating the story—revealing God's true nature and intentions. In Jesus, God shows humans up close what God is like and how God desires to work though us in the world.

The more Israel's history unfolds in the Bible, it seems like their image and understanding of God got more and more distorted. They tried to fit God into their understanding of what a god should do for them (like other cultures did that surrounded them). So, I believe, God decided that they (we) needed a much clearer picture of God; an undistorted image of God in three dimensions. More than just a cloud or fire or wind, God came and lived with humans in human form. This was God recalibrating the story—revealing God's true nature and intentions. In Jesus, God shows humans up close what God is like and how God desires to work though us in the world."

One of the biggest challenges we faced was that our group tended to focus on analyzing the stories rather than imagining them. This was especially surprising with our group because most of them were involved in creative endeavors—drama, music and the arts. What surfaced was that they were conditioned in school to focus on critical thinking skills all day long. It was a stretch for them to push beyond this way of thinking toward thinking more post-critically (beyond critical thinking). Instead of evaluating the plausibility of every detail in the story, we encouraged our group to dig deeper—to imagine and observe and place themselves in the story—to experience it, just like they would a good movie or novel.

One student shared, "I have never been asked to imagine anything in church before." This made me sad. Church should be a place where we continually explore our imaginations—faith in itself is an imaginative process; it is about taking that which is unseen and moving it into the deeper places of our lives.

This was a new challenge for me. Most all of the groups that I have worked with (even pastors!) did not struggle much to think imaginatively about the Bible. Rhythm was broken when my students stepped outside of the story to evaluate it—thereby distancing themselves from the story. So I tried out a new exercise to re-engage the group's imagination: "Close your eyes. Imagine you have a camera, and you are in the story we just told. As you replay the story in your mind, chose one part of this story to take a picture of. (Wait fifteen seconds.) Okay, do you have your picture? Please open your eyes. Who would like to share about your picture?"

This exercise seemed to help us focus on our experience of the story. Slowly we journeyed through all twelve stories over the course of six months. Along the way, our students began to engage with the stories more imaginatively. We gave each a blank sketchbook, asking them to draw their own version of the story symbols, and to capture with words and sketches what stood out to them from the story. Most of the students poured their thoughts and ideas into these. This really helped our students' engagement and ownership. One student created a collage on the cover of her journal representing her story.

A student shared a remarkable drawing of an eye with a reflection in the pupil of the burning Temple. She was reluctant to share verbally but was continually creating compelling sketches that (mostly) connected with story. Sitting next to her, a female student filled pages with her thoughts and insights, guardedly sharing only a few with the group. One session she shared, "The further we go I am seeing this story much clearer. I was struck today but how Jesus was impressed with the faith of the four friends who brought the man on the mat. Jesus noticed so many little details. He saw them through eyes of compassion. I want to be like that."

Another student followed the metaphor of a bird through the stories, creating beautiful drawings: a bird representing life in the garden, a bird as the messenger of safety to return to dry land after the flood, a bird as an expression of Solomon's wisdom, a bird perched in a in the tree that grew from a seed (Jesus' kingdom parable), and a bird as the Holy Spirit resting on Jesus. She even likened her faith to a "bird that is free to experience God."

This was (is) a thoughtful group, wrestling with complexities of the Bible and faith in ways that I had yet to see with high school students. They paid careful attention to the details of the characters in the stories. The further we went into the stories, the more I noticed them engaging in the process and digging in for meaning. One student shared, "It seems like the Temple was symbolic of the Israelites faith and relationship with God. They did not protect it and it was torn down. Then they longed to have it back."

Because of my students having such strong involvement in school and community drama groups, many were eager to read our second telling of the story. But it was still work to keep things on track. Jeanne, our associate pastor who co-led the group with me, did a good job of re-centering us. She reminded our group before some of the dialogue times, "Let's try to keep our discussion about *this* story—I know you get excited about connections you are making, but let's try not to bring in movies you've seen, Veggie Tales, anime, and concerns about the value of the Bible or the reality of God. Try to stay in the story, even if you need to come to it like you would other literature, okay?" (Some weeks I felt like my students would engage better if we were actually exploring stories from *The Hunger Games* instead of the Bible!)

After one Bible storying session, a student pulled me aside and said, "You said God will speak to us and illuminate something in the story. I haven't heard anything. Maybe God doesn't speak to me."

I was taken aback. Speechless. She seemed genuinely concerned— like she was left out by God. I collected my thoughts and said, "Well, I don't hear voices either! It is more of an inkling. A nudge. When you have been listening to these stories, or reading your Bible, have you ever had a part of the story jump out at you? Maybe it was an image, or word, or something said by a character in the story?"

She said, "I think so. I can't remember."

I continued, "Sometimes something in the Bible will stick with us. Pay attention to that. It could be something small–but sometimes it is the small things that God brings to mind. What you share matters, it helps us to see more about God."

"Hmm. I will keep listening and let you know."

The next week, I began by asking the group the same question I asked the student, "When you've been listening to these stories, have you ever had a part of the story seem to jump out at you? Maybe it was an image, or word, or something said by a character in the story?"

Most everyone in the group raised their hand.

"Even if that is something small, it is important. I think parts of these stories stand out to us for a reason—it's often God illuminating something to you. No one knows exactly how this works—it takes some faith to believe it. I do know that what you see in the story and share with this group matters. It may not seem meaningful to you, but it might reveal more about God to others in this group. Your observations are teaching me and showing me more about God each week."

Later, during the dialogue time, the girl who initially asked me about God speaking to her said, "I really connected with David in this story. It was like I could see him in the cave, singing to God. It made me not feel so alone."

A wide smile spread across my face and I felt the warmth of God's Spirit in our group in that moment.

I continued to ponder what it means to "hear" from God. Time and time again I have sensed guidance outside of myself. It is not an audible voice, but more of an inner whisper that stirs my conscience. It re-centers me, ringing true to the beauty of the compassionate Jesus. Often I sense this when hearing or reading a Bible story. It is like a part of the story hooks into me, speaking to a part of me that needs healing, encouragement or rest. I believe this is the Spirit of God remaking me, grafting me into the remarkable story or restoration that is a growing reality in our world. I will continue to listen for the gentle whisper of God each day, nudging me toward wholeness.

> It is like a part of the story hooks into me, speaking to a part of me that needs healing, encouragement or rest. I believe this is the Spirit of God remaking me, grafting me into the remarkable story or restoration that is a growing reality in our world.

"Go out and stand before me on the mountain," the Lord told him. And as Elijah stood there, the Lord passed by, and a mighty windstorm hit the mountain. It was such a terrible blast that the rocks were torn loose, but the Lord was not in the wind. After the wind there was an earthquake, but the Lord was not in the earthquake. And after the earthquake there was a fire, but the Lord was not in the fire. And after the fire there was the sound of a gentle whisper. When Elijah heard it, he wrapped his face in his cloak and went out and stood at the entrance of the cave.[1]

As we neared the end of our twelve-session experience with Bible storying, I asked this group of students to share how it connected to them. They said:

> I liked being able to use my imagination and see how the stories relate to my life.

> I see myself as part of a story that continues.

> It gave me a new perspective on the stories.

> I felt heard."

> I like the fact that I could sketch and put the story in pictures. It made it more relatable.

> I saw myself watching this story unfold. I saw how there is a message behind the stories.

This was a reminder that I had let go of my expectations and ego and realized that spiritual formation is the work of the Spirit—and cannot be predicted or produced from a process.

For most in the group it seemed to open up a wider avenue of accessibility to the Bible. For some, it was the first time they tried to find meaning in the Bible. These responses were not as momentous as some of the other responses I've heard in the past, but that doesn't matter. This was a reminder that I had let go of my expectations and ego and realized that spiritual formation is the work of the Spirit—and cannot be predicted or produced from a process. Bible storying doesn't release magic story dust that transforms every hearer. It doesn't yield specific results. It is so much more unpredictable and mystical than this.

Following our exploration of the Bible, we focused on telling our story—the story of our congregation and faith tradition. My congregation is a peace-church rooted in the Anabaptist tradition. We took several weeks to invite members of our congregation to tell their stories and dialogue about how their stories have meaning for us today. This is a practice that we continue, and we have seen it build meaningful connections and unique opportunities to learn about our church's story.

Merge

A few years ago, my brother Mark and I pulled together a team of youth workers and creative professionals to design an event that immersed teenagers in biblical narrative. The result is a unique event called Merge that helps students form a theological identity.

For six days, Merge uses Bible storying each morning to help high-schoolers explore key narratives from Creation to the Church. Each afternoon, youth groups participate in a group experience—an imaginative, hands-on, station-based activity that helps adolescents dig deeper into the Bible and discover meaning for their lives. Art and media, reflective activities, and interactive experiences propel teenagers toward creative responses to the stories each evening. Rooted in sound theology and proven experiential learning theory, Merge is designed to be a formational experience designed around helping the learner meet God and merge with God's restorative activity in the world. This event also serves as a great laboratory to try new and innovative approaches for spiritual formation. To find out more about Merge, go to **www.mergeevent.com**.

BIBLE STORYING AND CHILDREN'S MINISTRY

The responses to and interest in Bible storying that I have encountered have created in me a hunger to want to learn as much as I can about story, dialogue, spiritual formation and learning. This has become a lifelong pursuit. This hunger drove me to pursue a masters of education degree in integrated learning from Endicott College in Boston.

In my master's program, I was placed in a cohort of fourteen people, six of whom were Montessori educators. Through course study and the experiences of my classmates, I began to grow an appreciation for the Montessori approach to education. As I read and learned more about the founder, Dr. Maria Montessori, and her philosophy of education, it really resonated with me.

Dr. Montessori was one of the first women to become a licensed physician in Italy. In her work with developmentally challenged children, she came to believe that education was falsely based

> In the realm of spiritual formation, all are being formed. The teacher or leader is seeking the same essence as the student: to experience the divine, to grow in awareness of divine activity, to participate in community, and to be formed into a more compassionate person.

on the idea that children are empty vessels to be filled up by adults with knowledge. Conversely, she believed that with the right environment, materials and encouragement, every child could self-educate and "build" her or himself.[2] She stated, "the deepest longing of the child's soul—if he could only articulate it—would be expressed in just this way: 'Help me to help myself.'"[3] Montessori's first school began in 1907, and now there are more than eight thousand Montessori schools worldwide.[4] Montessori's belief in creating a fertile environment for learning cannot be overstated. She said, "It is the environment that educates, not the teacher directly; more precisely, it is the child's inherent formative energies, finding material in the environment to act upon purposefully, that calls or brings forth the child's true nature."[5]

This calls teachers to a different role. Montessori encouraged teachers to "follow the child,"[6] saying, "The teacher has thus become a director of the spontaneous work of the children. She is not a passive force, but a silent presence."[7] I identify with her assertion to respect a child's own journey and learn from the child, who has at least as much to offer us as we have to offer her or him. The best teachers are co-learners and students along with their class. Montessori's grandson, Mario, said, "love is the binding force" of education and a "a technique of love"[8] where teachers are to be an "observer-participant and active participant...based on mutual respect and confidence."[9]

In the realm of spiritual formation, all are being formed. The teacher or leader is seeking the same essence as the student: to experience the divine, to grow in awareness of divine activity, to participate in community, and to be formed into a more compassionate person. Leading in this way is an art, in which to succeed one must develop sensitivities of listening, noticing and empathy. Bible storying seems to be in step with this kind of leading and environment.

I soon discovered that many Christian spiritual formational approaches and resources were already developed that coincide with Montessori's approach to education. I was excited to explore these approaches and startled at how similar they were to how I was approaching Bible storying. The book Listening to Children on the Spiritual Journey, written by Dr. Scottie May and Dr. Catherine Stonehouse, seemed to tie these approaches together for me. May and Stonehouse's research and practices center on "Reflective Engagement," a term they use to "describe the approaches to ministry that flow from the work of biblical scholar Sofia Cavalletti." Cavalletti, along with Maria Montessori's assistant Gianna Gobbi, developed faith formation curricula called Catechesis of the Good Shepherd, which is rooted in Montessori principles.[10]

Cavalletti's work inspired many parallel curricula, including Jerome Berryman and Sonya Stewart's Godly Play and Young Children in Worship, Upper Room's The Way of the Child, and the work of Gretchen Wolff Pritchard.[11]

All of these curricula, described as "reflective engagement," move to create a calm, quiet, yet engaging place and share similar elements, such as:

› Telling a Bible story with minimum embellishment. For children, simple figures may be used to enact the narrative. Participants are asked to use their imagination to sense the story and place themselves as an eyewitness.

› Reflecting on the story during moments of silence.

› Wondering about the story aloud through statements and questions.

› Responding to the story through a choice of expressions, including: art, reenactment, re-listening to the story, contemplative reading, and journaling.

› Sharing observations during group dialogue, guided by open-ended questions.[12]

Teachers of this method are encouraged to embrace a role to "simply set the stage for boys and girls to listen to God, talk to God, meet, and come to know God." May and Stonehouse found that through reflective engagement, "Children gave us a glimpse of their spiritual potential, how they were at work putting together pieces of theological understandings, how they experienced God."[13]

In my quest to improve Bible storying and learn from the wealth of experience in these approaches, I have connected with Dr. May. She agrees that Bible storying is in the "reflective engagement" family. Dr. May has allowed me to share about Bible storying in her seminary class and has encouraged me to develop resources for children with this approach. So, I began a few years ago, and continue to experiment with Bible storying with children.

My area of practical experience is largely in youth ministry, so I sought partners who were practitioners of children's ministry. I built lasting relationships with a few people willing to integrate Bible storying into their children's ministries. Not only did they adapt some of the unpublished curriculum I developed, they guided me in the development and improvement of some of my beta materials. Here are some comments from a few of those key partners:

> Once we began storying, our whole children's ministry went through a tremendous spiritual transformation. We shifted from absorbing information about God and the Bible to creating a sacred space for God to transform us through imaginative listening and responding to God's word.
> —REBEKAH LOWE, CHILDREN'S MINISTER FROM SOUTHERN CALIFORNIA

> I started using Bible storying with "children" of all ages. Soon, parents were coming to me wondering what I was teaching their kids: "My children keep talking to me about what the Holy Spirit is teaching them. I know it is not coming from me." Families started meeting together and doing community around Bible storying. Michael Novelli has ventured with me into unknown territories as we wrestled with how this can be done with children and families throughout the world. As you read and practice what is in this book, be prepared for God to turn your world upside down. He did it to me!
> —GARY STRUDLER, CHILDREN AND FAMILY PASTOR IN PORTLAND, OREGON

We worked with Michael when he was in the 'beta phase' of much of the storying effort. It was extremely well received by everyone from our Early Childhooders up through our Adult Small Groups. I was amazed at how it captured the attention of any age group and transported them into the story as they engaged in imaginative listening. I was even more amazed at what they discovered for themselves and how the Holy Spirit used this method and these stories to move them toward a deeper understanding of God's story, their part in that story, and what they should do as a result.
—MARC FRY, FAMILY PASTOR FROM BOLLINGBROOK, ILLINOIS

These friends, along with Dr. Leon Blanchette from Olivet Nazerene University (see Dr. Blanchette's True Story about storying in this chapter), have taken this approach, expanded and implemented it in amazing ways. I am learning so much from them! There certainly is a growing interest in Bible storying with children. My hope is that in the future I will be able to invest more in these partnerships and finish developing resources for children and families.

BIBLE STORYING WITH ADULTS AND BETWEEN GENERATIONS

Over the last several years, I have had the privilege of seeing Bible storying used in a variety of contexts. Many churches have contacted me expressing how this approach is connecting well with their adult small groups. Others have integrated it into preaching. I met with one group of small group leaders who were leading a group of seventy- to eighty-year-olds!

A growing application of Bible storying that I find intriguing is with intergenerational groups. A few churches have shared with me their efforts to create "extended family" groups that use storying as one of the central learning tools. My encouragement to these churches was to focus on conversation, using less questions and a slightly more basic storying structure. The emphasis should be on storying with and not to children and youth. As much as possible, everyone should participate as equals, considering the questions, sharing, wondering, drawing or writing and so on.

Even though intergenerational approaches to ministry are not new, many churches are now (re)entering this conversation and wondering how they might draw every one together toward shared vision and experience of spiritual growth. Though slow-moving for most congregations, the pendulum seems to be is swinging away from highly segmented, top-down approaches to faith formation, toward equipping families and smaller groups to be hubs of spiritual growth. I wonder if the future of effective spiritual formation will center in intergenerational ministry? Let me attempt to paint a picture of this:

> Spiritual formation is about a community building a culture of care, learning, acceptance and sacrifice. What if our picture of community extended beyond a peer group of friends, to an extended family—a tribe—a table . . . gathering together with young and old to share life and grow together through our diversity of thought and experiences, striving to become a spiritual family?

> Building a culture—a family—like this cannot happen on a large scale. It calls us into deeper relationships—to be known and to know others and discover the depths of Christ together. True intergenerational ministry (like all true ministry) must have a life beyond strategy, programing and models—it must be an incarnation. It is entering into life alongside one another, sometimes spontaneously.

> Faith will thrive when sparked by the honesty, humility, struggle and faithfulness of those close to us. We are carried by the faith stories of those younger and older than us. Diversity of thought and perspectives is fuel for our growth.

> Intergenerational extended families could be incubators for us to explore our common story and identity. Central to our experience could be learning about the Biblical story, group involvement and dialogue, prayer and ritual.

> An intergenerational community should be marked by a profound level of acceptance. It must be a place where we know we will always be wanted, heard and loved. This

is especially vital for adolescents in the midst of a crisis of identity and faith. If questions, doubts and wonderings are invited (and celebrated!) it will usher in a sense of deep belonging. Adults must create a culture of listening and encouragement, modeling how they genuinely learn from every person—especially from children and teenagers.

For many of us in North America, this picture of an extended spiritual family seems strange or idealistic. If you are like me, many of your experiences with intergenerational church ministry felt awkward or forced. Youth "involvement" in church services and ministry often comes across as a token showcase of talents, accomplishments or piety to sooth parent angst. The importance of intergenerational ministry is more than just reaching youth or creating another category of programs—I believe it is vital to helping people grow and thrive in their faith for the long haul.

Together, I think we must experiment with "extended spiritual families" as places of faith formation where people of every age can connect and grow. Bible storying could be an important approach that is accessible and scalable to reach all ages at the same time.

BIBLE STORYING RESOURCES

My journey with Bible storying was born out of a desire to help my students connect with the Bible. It grew into Echo the Story, a ministry to help churches connect with the Bible through storying. But I realized that in order to best help churches, I needed support. I could not finish the story sets and resources that people were asking for on my own. I had developed iterations of different story sets from seven to thirty-six Bible stories, and multiyear scope-and-sequence plans, but I lacked the time or resources to be able to invest in completing these so others could use them. So I began to explore ways in which I could partner with others in order to serve more people. In 2011 I began conversations with sparkhouse, the ecumenical division of Augsburg Fortress Publishers. Our shared passion to pioneer new and creative resources for churches was obvious. The sparkhouse team loved what Echo had been doing, and desired to expand the impact of Bible storying to reach even more people. So when sparkhouse offered to acquire Echo the Story, I was thrilled to accept.

In 2012 we started envisioning how Echo's art of Bible storying and sparkhouse's innovative approaches to spiritual formation could join together to connect more people with a vibrant, growing faith. Now, I have been given the amazing opportunity to do what I love and work on the talented team at sparkhouse. Together we are creating a new family of Echo resources for your church community. The first resource was released in June of 2013, a twelve-story overview of the Bible. Exciting things are ahead!

QUESTIONS FOR REFLECTION AND DISCUSSION

> *Which parts of this chapter relate to your own story?*

> *What is motivating you to try new approaches to teaching?*

> *What expectations do you have for your ministry or small group? How are ministry expectations sometimes harmful? How might they be helpful?*

> *What experiences have you had with alternative approaches to education (like Montessori)?*

> *In what contexts do you think Bible storying would be effective? What ages do you think would best connect with this approach?*

A TRUE STORY ABOUT STORYING

Life as a children's pastor and professor of Christian education has led to an interesting journey of trying to discover the "best" methodology for leading children into an intimate relationship with Christ. On that journey, I have discovered and implemented a variety of approaches in an attempt to find that one pedagogy that both fit my philosophy of ministry and worked pragmatically in local church ministry. Serving now as a full-time professor and part-time children's pastor, I have had the opportunity to investigate the topic with vigor and intentionality. Through that investigation, I discovered two separate, but similar approaches to ministry that have intrigued me: Godly Play and Catechesis of the Good Shepherd. These two liturgical-type approaches challenged the approach to ministry that I most commonly used. While I resonated with the approaches to ministry, even though the concepts were new, I realized that both of these approaches dealt with preschoolers and were usually in a small church setting. I began to wonder if a similar approach might work with elementary age children and in a larger church context. So I began the journey of what this approach might look like under different conditions.

As I continued on my journey, the day came that I discovered *Shaped by the Story* by Michael Novelli. As I read Michael's book I began to realize that we spoke a similar language. This discovery led to several phone conversations with Michael and an eventual invitation to share "The Story" with my children's ministry class. As we listened to him describe and share the journey he was leading his youth on, I began to ask the same question I had asked earlier in this journey, "What would this look like with elementary age children in a larger church context?"

So a new journey began with the children of my church as we began to implement the meta-narrative approach that Michael was proposing. With his permission, we began to use the curriculum that he had developed for his youth. With a tweak here and there, and customizing the approach to fit the cognitive and spiritual development of children, we were off and running. In our first six months, we covered the entire meta-narrative from creation to the return of Christ by highlighting key stories. Each of the stories was represented with a picture (provided by Michael) that helped the children remember the major focus of the story. To this day our children can name the 24 major stories of the meta-narrative.

As my journey with this approach to ministry has continued, many adjustments to the way we experienced worship have been made. One of my key discoveries that built on what I had learned from Michael came from two ladies that have become my heroes in ministry; Drs. Catherine Stonehouse and Scottie May. Through their writings and one-on-one discussions I came across what is commonly referred to as "storying" or "story forming." The concept was originally developed by Maria Montessori and Sophia Cavalletti, but more recently adapted by Jerome Berryman. The basic idea is to tell the story in such a way that the child lives in the story and experiences the Story personally. Children are then asked open-ended questions about the Story. Sometimes these questions are referred to as "I wonder..." questions. This approach honors the role of the Holy Spirit in the lives of children and allows the child to live in the Story; to make the Story their own.

I'm sure my journey is not over. I suspect that I will continue to discover ways to help the Story of God become real in the lives of children. As this process continues to develop, I will always be in debt and grateful to Michael for his part in challenging me to reconsider the model by which I conducted ministry for years. His books have been a tremendous help on my journey.

—**LEON BLANCHETTE**, ED.D., PROFESSOR OF CHRISTIAN EDUCATION
  OLIVET NAZARENE UNIVERSITY

PART **TWO**

why Bible storying connects

CHAPTER SIX

THE POWER OF STORIES

> Story is our brightest hope. Story is the heart of our language capacity . . . story heals, reminds and guides us. Story is the most powerful tool ever granted ordinary people. Story is power.
>
> –CHRISTINA BALDWIN[1]

Bible storying has given me first-hand experience of the power of stories to shape lives. But why? What is it about the narrative form that connects better than other forms of communication? Aren't facts and propositions more clear and concise?

Take a moment and think about a favorite story from your childhood. It could be a family story that was passed down or a story from a book. Who told you this story? What did you like about it? Who was your favorite character?

Now, think about one of your favorite stories today. It could be from a movie or novel—whatever pops into your mind first. What is interesting about this story? How does the story make you feel? How do you relate to the story?

HOW STORIES HOOK US IN

Stories engage us in profound ways. In *Christ Plays in Ten Thousand Places*, author Eugene Peterson writes:

> Story is the most natural way of enlarging and deepening our sense of reality, and then enlisting us as participants in it. Stories open doors to areas or aspects of life that we didn't know were there, or had quit noticing out of over-familiarity, or supposed were out-of-bounds to us. They then welcome us in. Stories are verbal acts of hospitality.[2]

Stories invite us into their reality by capturing our imaginations and invoking our emotion and empathy. How many times has a movie, a book, or a song made you feel something deep and moving—something you couldn't even describe? Stories draw us in and we begin to feel what the characters feel. Their pain becomes our pain; their victory becomes our victory. We enter stories and make them part of our experience. We step inside the story and relate the characters and events to our own experiences.

> The ability of stories to carry us into another world is an associative capacity; it is our brain relating the characters and details of the story to our own experiences.

Stories lure us into an immersive state that psychologists call "narrative transport."[3] Inwardly we are transported to another place. Stories do this with psychological realism, depicting recognizable emotions and believable interactions among characters.[4]

Brain scientist Paul Zak found that even the simplest narrative can elicit powerful empathic response by triggering the release of neurochemicals like cortisol (prompting distress) and oxytocin (prompting empathy). He said, "stories are powerful because they transport us into other people's worlds but, in doing that, they change the way our brains work and potentially change our brain chemistry."[5]

The ability of stories to carry us into another world is an associative capacity; it is our brain relating the characters and details of the story to our own experiences. Renowned authors and brain researchers Tony and Barry Buzan describe the connections our brains make with stories like this: "Each bit of information entering your brain—every sensation, memory, or thought—can be represented as a central sphere from which radiate tens, hundreds, thousands, millions of hooks. Each hook represents an association, and each association as its own infinite array of links and connections."[6]

Because stories are so emotive and imaginative, they are like Velcro, containing a myriad of hooks that easily latch to our experiences. Every sensory experience stored in our brains can be recalled and reassociated with a story. So it's true, stories do literally *hook you in* (rim shot)!

WHOLE-BRAIN BENEFITS

Stories connect with and stimulate our brains more than any other form of communication. During a Library of Congress lecture, Dr. Robert Ornstein, a leading psychologist and professor at Stanford, said:

> Stories are designed to embody—in their characters, plots, and imagery—patterns and relationships that nurture a part of the mind that's unreachable in more direct ways, thus increasing our understanding and breadth of vision, in addition to fostering our ability to think critically. Stories activate the right side of the brain much more than reading normal prose. The right side of the brain provides "context," the essential function of putting together the different components of experience. The left side provides the "text," or the pieces themselves.[7]

A growing emphasis on narrative and story is now being used in education in North America. Current educational research has shown that the use of narrative (across subject matter) has had very positive effects, such as

> Sparking creativity and increasing engagement

> Developing listening skills

> Increasing comprehension

> Improving literacy, writing and language mastery

> Making information much more memorable

> Building a sense of community and involvement

> Strengthening logical and critical thinking skills[8]

No other medium addresses varied learning styles like storytelling does. Educators are realizing that stories can be used as a powerful and memorable vehicle to convey content. Many creative approaches are being used to implement narrative in schools today. My wife has used stories in her elementary classroom to help connect math to real-life scenarios, and she found that this approach worked much more effectively than conventional methods for teaching math concepts.

In an article entitled "'Hamlet' Too Hard? Try a Comic Book," Teresa Méndez, staff writer for *The Christian Science Monitor*, writes, "At Oneida High School in upstate New York, Diane Roy teaches students who failed ninth-grade English the first time around. Last year, on the heels of Hamlet, she presented her class with a graphic novel—essentially a variety of comic book. . . . Each student was required to read five graphic novels. 'There wasn't a single student in this class of kids— nonreaders who don't enjoy reading—who didn't read double that number,' Roy says. 'They would read them overnight . . . they were reading them at lunch, in the hallway.'"[9]

> No other medium addresses varied learning styles like storytelling does.

Graphic novels use a combination of media—images and words—to connect students to a story in a new way. Japanese graphic novels, called manga, have become hugely popular with young readers and are now becoming bestsellers among teenagers in the United States.

THE STRUCTURE OF STORY

We intuitively know what stories are, especially those that move us. But what exactly is a story? My favorite simple definition is from author Donald Miller: "A story is essentially this: a character that wants something and overcomes conflict to get it."[10] Characters are critical to a story, they are required to make it relatable, compelling and meaningful. But what happens to the characters—rising and falling actions, intentions, struggles, and details—are what make up a good story.

Professional storyteller Kendall Haven reminds us that "a story is a 'thing,' a specific narrative structure. It is a framework—a narrative architechture. Story is not the content, but the scaffolding upon which some content (fiction or nonfiction) is hung."[11] So what is the structure of a good story? Most good stories have a beginning, middle and end, rising action, conflict points, a climax, and a resolution. Below is an example of a Story Map to provide visual scaffolding of the structure of a story. I've also included a Story Map Activity in appendix c for your to chart a Bible story using this structure.

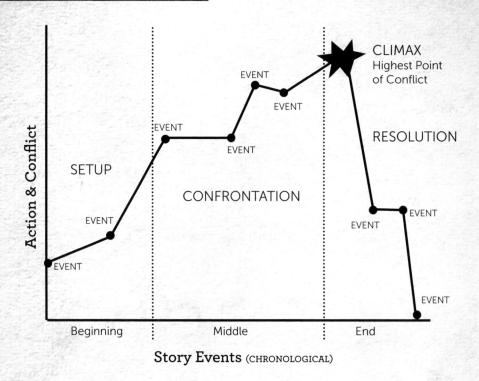

Story Events (CHRONOLOGICAL)

I have also created a simple story activity called a Story Spine.
I found this helpful in writing short stories and evaluating the
effectiveness of stories. This is the Story Spine I have been using:

Once upon a time . . . Each day . . . But one day . . . Because of that . . .
(repeat a few times or as needed)
Until finally . . . Ever since then . . .

Try this out and create a simple story!

WIRED FOR STORY

Each person is born with the innate ability to learn and share
through stories. By the time most children are three years old, they
can tell many kinds of stories, recall stories they've heard, and even
make up their own stories. Story is ingrained in us and is a critical
part of our development.

Author Christina Baldwin wrote, "We live in story like a fish lives
in water. We swim through words and images siphoning story

through our minds the way a fish siphons water through its gills ... we cannot process experience without story. We are the story-making creatures."[12] Educator Sherelle Walker affirms that stories are a part of our natural brain processes: "While stories often have a profound effect on us due to emotional content, recent research also shows that our brains are actually hard-wired to seek out a coherent narrative structure in the stories we hear and tell. This structure helps us absorb the information in a story, and connect it with our own experiences in the world."[13]

When children listen to stories, they respond by imagining the characters and places described by the words in their minds. According to psychologist Jerome Bruner, children "turn things into stories, and when they try to make sense of their life they use the storied version of their experience as the basis for further reflection. If they don't catch something in a narrative structure, it doesn't get remembered very well, and it doesn't seem to be accessible for further kinds of mulling over."[14]

> We are story-minded beings. Instinctively, we filter life into stories to provide structure, context and relevance in our minds.

As adults, we continue to translate our experiences and memories into stories. Kendall Haven describes this translation: "Human minds use a specific story structure to impose order onto incoming narrative and experiential information. . . . These techniques are employed at the automatic, subconscious level."[15]

We are story-minded beings. Instinctively, we filter life into stories to provide structure, context and relevance in our minds. Kendall Haven supports this notion, stating: "Results from a dozen prominent congnitive sceintists and developmental psychologists have confirmed that human minds *do* rely on stories and on story architechture as the primary roadmap for understanding, making sense of, remember and planning our lives."[16]

Stories provide a framework for our lives; they order our memories and assign value to our experiences. Therapist Lewis Mehl-Madrona desribes the depth and importance that stories provide us: "Stories hold a richness and complexity that simple declarative facts can never grasp . . . Story provides the dominant frame for organizing experience and for creating meaning out of experience."[17]

STORY SHAPES IDENTITY

Throughout history, societies have passed on their values, beliefs, and traditions through stories. Woven into the fabric of our cultures, families, and communities, they're the strands that bind us together. Christina Baldwin noted: "Life hangs on a narrative thread. This thread is a braid of stories that inform us about who we are, and where we come from, and where we might go."

Stories define who we are. Story is at the core of our identities and is the essence of our memories. Stories are the containers of culture and faith. Kendall Haven wrote that, "Stories are our universal storehouses of knowledge, beliefs, values, attitiudes, passions, dreams imagination, and vision."[18] He continued, "Stories facilitate emergent social selves, relational identities, and co-cultural understanding."[19]

Story has the remarkable power to stir our intellect and emotions, move us toward empathy, order our memories and experiences, and shape our identities and dreams. Gordon Chalmers exclaimed, "The rarest and mightiest possession of the human spirit can be discovered only by means of a story and by no other process of thinking."[20]

QUESTIONS FOR REFLECTION AND DISCUSSION

> *What stories have shaped your life?*

> *What important family stories have been told to you? What family stories have you passed on?*

> *Why do you think that stories shape us more than other forms of communication?*

> *How might you incorporate more storytelling in your ministry?*

A TRUE STORY ABOUT STORYING

Storying isn't for the faint of heart. It's unpredictable. It's chaotic. It exposes what your students really believe. It takes effort. You can't control it, but you must be confident in it. But for the brave, storying yields huge benefits. My high schoolers love the process. They appreciate the respect of having their voices heard in a meaningful way, and when they spew out weird ideas, storying gives them a safe environment in which to explore their thoughts and learn to think theologically. At first I worried about what would happen if they came to the wrong conclusions or gave wrong answers. But it's been amazing to see communal correcting at work and to see how one or two questions will get them to bounce their thoughts off the story or the rest of the group. Here are the three biggest benefits I've seen: no matter how much or how little Bible knowledge a person has, everyone is placed on the same level. Students learn to think theologically in a safe environment and to distinguish between things they've heard about God's story and what's actually in God's story. Students see the Bible as one connected story to live out of and into.

—JOSH MILLER, YOUTH WORKER IN GENEVA, ILLINOIS

CHAPTER SEVEN

DISSECTING & DISTILLING

> Rather than coming at a passage as an isolated event from
> which we will extract a moral saying, or trying to pull a few
> words to build a case, we see the character and movement
> of God in a dance with his people. We see God wooing
> and engaging and saving and guiding and disciplining . . .
> all in order to bring restoration and reconciliation to a world
> he loves. In this way we now have a story, our story, from
> which to engage the world.[1]
> —JEN WISE

A STORY-SHAPED CULTURE

Stories shape culture. Throughout the world, cultural narratives are
embedded with values, beliefs, and visions that emerge from the
communities that tell them. Each has the power to shape thoughts,
actions, and worldviews. Media strategist Andrea Phillips blogged,
"stories are the truths a society believes in . . . the stories we see and
hear influence how we see the world. Story is the engine that drives
culture. That means that changing any aspect of culture requires
telling new stories."[2] I believe that the prevailing story currently
dominating Western cultures is the story of consumerism. This
story is marked by a drive for wealth, self-interest and advancement,
and acquisition. The influence of economic dominance seems to
reach every facet of American life.

The underlying goals of the consumeristic story are individual
prosperity, success and status, power, comfort, and security. The
allure of this story, sometimes called the American dream, is that
if you work hard you can become self-sufficient and entitled to a
privileged, carefree, perfect life. Happiness comes through acquiring
more possessions, comfortable living, luxury, and entertainment.

AN INDUSTRIAL COMPLEX

The messages of consumerism are difficult to avoid; they come in many different forms and are displayed seemingly everywhere we look. Advertisements are crafted by some the world's most creative minds, dazzling us through sight and sound, tugging on hearts (and wallets) through captivating narratives that try to tell us what we need and who we are. Through compelling and emotive storylines, advertising tells us that we should be dissatisfied with who we are and what we have—that we are incomplete. But they also provide a solution—a product or service that will bring completion and happiness—if we order now.

Phillips writes, "For many long decades, our culture has been held fast in the grip of media owned by a privileged few. Television networks, film studios, and publishers alone held the power to make culture. Not to mention commercials, little stories in between the stories, suggesting that happiness lies forever just at your fingertips, waiting only for you to buy the next phone or car or lipstick."[3]

> Through compelling and emotive storylines, advertising tells us that we should be dissatisfied with who we are and what we have—that we are incomplete.

Educator Brian Swimme describes how advertisements target children early in life:

Before a child enters first grade science class, and before entering in any real way into our religious ceremonies, a child will have soaked in thirty-thousand advertisements. The time our teenagers spend absorbing ads is more than their total stay in high school. Advertisement is where our children receive their basic grasp of the world's meaning, which amounts to their primary religious faith, though unrecognized as such....The fact that consumerism has become the dominant world-faith is largely invisible to us, so it is helpful to understand clearly that to hand our children over to the consumer culture is to place them in the care of the planet's most sophisticated religious preachers.[4]

Describing consumerism as the "dominant world-faith" is jarring to me. It causes me to reflect on how this story is shaping my life and family. It reveals to me how I have tried (with much dissonance) to blend consumerism with my own beliefs and faith. In his book *Education for Human Development*, psychologist Mario Montessori, Jr. narrated how the consumeristic story and drive toward industrialization are affecting human identity:

> God created man in His image, and man created machines in his image. The machines are now reshaping man, and God has been declared dead; the guiding and unifying principle in human existence has been eliminated. The individual is being deprived of his share in shaping his personal destiny; his life is being determined, more and more, by impersonal institutions and technological devices that keep him in bondage. Meaning and identity are being lost in the process; anxiety and a growing feeling of disorientation, futility, helplessness, and frustration are taking over. In the circumstances, revolt is the only way the individual can recover his rights as man.[5]

The progression of the consumeristic story has driven Western cultures toward a mechanized and manufactured way of living, delivered through technology. Transportation, clothing, communication, entertainment, and even food are processed and produced in factories by machines. Montessori is imploring us to consider a better story than the pursuit of a dehumanizing consumeristic endeavor.

Don't misunderstand the point—I'm not saying we need to rid ourselves of all the modern advancements and board a horse and buggy to yesteryear. We benefit from the development of science, technology and medicine every day. I believe that in many ways this progress has made our lives better. It is the commodification of most every aspect of life that is an empty pursuit.

THE SWAY OF CONSUMERISM

Every facet of culture has been permeated by the consumeristic story. Education has been shaped by this story, viewing students as collectors of information with the goal that this will translate into knowledge and skills to build a workforce to increase economic endeavors. Schools built competitive environments that focused on analytical, rote, and repetitive work. Educator Philip Gang describes how the goal of industrialization has shaped the form of education in America: "Nowhere is the mechanistic age more conspicuous than in the field of education where knowledge is separated into fixed categories and is parceled out in assembly-line fashion. The school favors competition over cooperation and achievement over integration. Modeled after the factory, mechanistic age schools have a covert curriculum in punctuality, obedience, and rote repetitive work."[6]

> What seems to be surfacing is an underlying (perhaps unintentional) belief that meaning, faith, and God may be found in facts.

My concern is that the overarching philosophy for American education is operating on a model of the past and not the future, treating students as cogs in a machine rather than lives to be invest into. Religious institutions follow suit in their educational endeavors, taking on much of the philosophy and form of Western public education.

As with public education, the focus in much of Christian education is on the accumulation of information and facts. Some churches have adopted the modern mantra "knowledge is power." This has translated to equate cognitive adherence to a set of propositions that meet the requirement for membership, faith, and a relationship with God. What seems to be surfacing is an underlying (perhaps unintentional) belief that meaning, faith, and God may be found in facts.

Without question, Christian churches have been swayed by the influence of the story of consumerism. Many American churches seem to believe that they must sell their message through compelling marketing, plush facilities, professional programs, innovative technology, and entertainment spectacles. Congregants are treated as consumers seeking products and services to meet their spiritual needs. If a church does not meet their particular tastes or style, they simply shop for a new one. Church-hoppers will trade-up to a church that has better amenities (a coffee bar or soft theater-style seating) and programs (feel-good sermons or a "kidz playworld"). Community and service are compartmentalized to try to fit age, stage, and affinity, then scheduled and squeezed into overbooked lives and common interests.

This brand of faith leaves many, like myself, wanting more. Instead of church being a body—a interconnected community of deep relationships—it feels disembodied. Programs and proclamation take center stage over relationships. Instead of church feeling like a living, *incarnational* family of faith,. it feels *uncarnational*. Little space is given for being present with one another and with the divine. I go to a church rather than be the church. It is about me rather than us.

I think the dissonance many feel with "consumer church" is guiding us toward a better story. It is reminding us that the way of Jesus is an alternative story that is not compatible with many of our cultural stories. Jesus embodied and ushered in way of life—a gospel, a story—that stands in contrast to the crippling story of consumerism and the dominant epic of empire.

Author Stephen Shoemaker said in his book *GodStories*, "Our lives must find their place in some greater story or they will find their place in some lesser story. Our contemporary postmodern world is a world of a thousand stories and a thousand gods. And these stories become splintered images, brilliant, excitable, beautiful perhaps, but separated from any larger narrative to give them meaning and truth."[7] Thankfully, God, through Jesus, offers us a greater story.

CERTAINTY AND CONTROL

The consumeristic story has been brewing for thousands of years. It is rooted in an anthropocentric view that leads humans to refuse to accept limits imposed from without—or even from within— their own being. The influence of preeminent philosophers have helped to shaped human thinking toward this mechanistic perspective: Francis Bacon exalted knowledge as power; Galileo Galilei asserted that nature is written in the language of mathematics; and Rene Descartes employed us to break every dilemma into its constituent parts, to divide and subdivide until an answer is found through analysis. Building on this line of thought, Western cultures constructed a worldview in which the role of humanity is to strive for clarity, control, and certainty.

So, this perspective has also been applied to the Bible, using the tools of science—analysis, segmentation, and dissection—to try to uncover intention. Theologians are trained to be like forensic scientists, examining the Bible to uncover the original authors' singular intended meaning using hermeneutical methods, testing and retesting hypotheses.

> It seems that coming to the Bible with a purely analytical perspective creates distance; we must stand apart from the whole to dissect, evaluate and categorize. Dissection also seems to assume that the subject is dead.

Without question, there is an immense value in studying the history, context, and etymology of the Bible. I rely on the work of scholars and these approaches and tools every day. These tools are tremendous assets in helping us to reengage with the biblical story in deeper ways. But my concern is that we get fixated on these tools, believing that if we dig deep enough and understand more contextually, we will somehow uncover the author's true intentions and thereby have the definitive, correct interpretation. We seek to become masters of the text, believing that we will arrive at biblical rightness, control, and certainty. But most often, certainty is an illusion, and the Bible only becomes as useful as our knowledge of history.

It seems that coming to the Bible with a purely analytical perspective creates distance; we must stand apart from the whole to dissect, evaluate, and categorize. Dissection also seems to assume that the subject is dead. It focuses on realm of the rational and didactic, losing sight of the realm of Spirit and intuition and faith. For me, the Bible is a living book, one that is neither tamable nor needs to be tamed. The beauty of it is that it is a living story that God uses to reveal newness and truth to us at every turn.

SCATTERED PIECES

The dissect-and-distill mindset and approach to the Bible has been passed down from pastors and theologians to everyday churchgoers. From the time I was a teen through my late twenties, I was not aware that there was another way to come to the Bible. In *The Second Coming of the Church*, researcher George Barna writes:

> For years we have been exposing Christians to scattered, random bits of biblical knowledge through our church services and Christian education classes. They hear a principle here and read a truth there, then nod their head in approval and feel momentarily satisfied over receiving this new insight into their faith. But within the space of just a few hours that principle or truth is lost in the busy-ness and complexity of their lives. They could not capture that insight and own it because they have never been given sufficient context and method that would enable them to analyze, categorize, and utilize the principle or truth.[8]

To make the Bible more palatable and usable, pastors use their training in the science of distillation, breaking down it down into major points and themes. They learn how to propositionalize and conceptualize the Bible in an effort to make it clear—and to support his or her idea or points. As I alluded to earlier in this book, preachers become like momma birds feeding their young—digesting the Bible then regurgitating it back to our congregants in bite-size pieces, hoping they take its nourishment—and don't spew it back on us!

Noted children's ministry expert Ivy Beckwith, in her book *Formational Children's Ministry*, points to the emergence of this approach in preaching:

> In the seventeenth and eighteenth centuries, with the age of Enlightenment and the birth of modernism, things changed. Scriptures were seen to refer to something behind the text that could be excavated from it through the application of a proper rational method. The Bible became, in effect, more than a story. Theologian John Wright explains,

"The bible became a source, not a text. Theologians and preachers understood the Scriptures as a platform on which they could either access experiences of the divine or build systems of proposition to nurture the life of their congregations and call unbelievers to faith."[9]

Beckwith goes on to say, "we need to really understand that Bible stories are not vehicles for getting us to propositional truth about God. Bible stories are already truth about God. Let's let the story be the story and tell its own truth to us."[10]

PROVERBIALIZING AND FABLEIZING

As I do workshops and consult churches, I continually talk with pastors who staunchly defend preaching as sacred and the proper proclamation of the truth of the Bible. Preaching is most often the presentation of concepts that are undergirded by Scriptures. They are using the Bible as a platform, a source. This is not necessarily wrong to do, and is an inspiring art in itself, but it is questionable to defend as sacred.

> **Most (one-directional) forms of preaching subtly translate the notion that the Bible should only be handled by those who are highly trained professionals.**

Of concern is that most (one-directional) forms of preaching subtly translate the notion that the Bible should only be handled by those who are highly trained professionals. Conversely, Bible study—personal and cooperate—are championed as required for growth as a Christian. So our congregants try to adopt the same process to their Bible reading that we model from the pulpit (and is modeled in most Bible study curricula).

The version of the dissect-and-distill process that has been passed down by us (church leadership) is a "lite" version—it does not carry with it a deep regard for biblical or historical context that the (ministry) professional version aspires to. Chapters and verses were imposed on the scriptures to help us with this process of dissection.

Barna stated:

> Bible reading has become the religious equivalent of
> sound-bite journalism. When people read from the Bible
> they typically open it, read a brief passage without much
> regard for the context, and consider the primary thought or
> feeling that the passage provided. If they are comfortable
> with it, they accept it; otherwise, they deem it interesting
> but irrelevant to their life, and move on. There is shockingly
> little growth evident in people's understanding of the
> fundamental themes of the scriptures and amazingly little
> interest in deepening their knowledge and application of
> biblical principles.[11]

We skim the Bible like a self-help book, looking for bite-size moral quips and handy life lessons.

We have been conditioned to come to the Bible to find something useful and valuable for our personal lives, like a prospector panning for gold. If we sift enough, we will find a nugget of truth that seems useful or applicable to us; then we ascribe our own meaning to it. I call this approach proverbializing—treating the Bible like it is just a collection of proverbs. Ivy Beckwith calls this the "Aesop-fableization" of the Bible.[12] We skim the Bible like a self-help book, looking for bite-size moral quips and handy life lessons. Professor of theology at Taylor Seminary Barbara Horkoff Mutch equates this skimming to informational reading and proposes a more formational approach to the Bible:

> Reading for information is characterized by an attempt
> to cover as much text as possible as quickly as possible.
> It attempts to master the text and is primarily critical and
> characterized by a problem-solving mentality. While there is
> certainly a place for this type of reading, too often we come
> to Scripture with a utilitarian approach, in order to "get
> something for the day" or to deliver a message to others.[13]

In contrast, reading for formation focuses on the quality rather than the quantity of reading. It is characterized by the intention of meeting God in the text. When we are reading for formation, we seek depth. We desire to respond to what we read and to conform our lives to the patterns revealed in the actions and the character of the God we follow and love. We give up our efforts to master the text, and we place ourselves in a posture that remains open to mystery. Reading for formation involves a loving, humble sitting with Scripture, characterized by patience and hope.

The dominance of analytical approaches to the Bible has caused us to lose our way. As we fragment and propositionalize the Scriptures, we strip it of its narrative power. It becomes confusing, dull, and impotent. We lose sight of the overarching story and its characters.

We must begin to come to the Bible with both eyes open—with stereoscopic vision. This means moving beyond (but not leaving behind) the myopic lens of modernity that analyzes with a microscope and gets lost in the minutia. To create balance, our other eye—the eye that gives us a sense of Scripture's mystery and multivalence—may need to become dominant for a while. This eye gives us an imaginative lens to discover another dimension of the Bible and experience it as our own story.

STORY LENS

The first time I realized that the Bible has a narrative framework was at the workshop I attended with John Witte. This was twelve years into my vocational ministry. Why had I never been awakened to the reality that 75 percent of the Bible is in the form of a narrative? Looking at the Bible through the lens of narrative has opened an entirely new world to me. It has reinvigorated my desire to read and find myself within the pages of the Bible. Eugene H. Peterson, translator of *The Message*, describes it this way:

> Stories are the most prominent biblical way of helping us see ourselves in "the God story," which always gets around to the story of God making and saving us. Stories, in contrast to abstract statements of truth, tease us into becoming participants in what is being said. We find ourselves involved in the action. We may start as spectators or critics, but if the story is good (and the biblical stories are very good!), we find ourselves no longer just listening to but inhabiting the story.[14]

We're called to live in a story that's still unfurling. God is not finished with us yet, thankfully. The Bible story is not just a story from the past; it's a living story, one of vibrancy and dimension. It's incarnational, entering our lives differently than other stories can. God calls us to inhabit the story, allowing it to shape and guide our lives.

Richard Jensen puts it this way:

> The stories of the Bible invite us to participate in their reality . . . not to understand that reality. Participating in the reality of the gospel in story form is something quite different than understanding the gospel in idea form. The fact that we participate in the life of stories means that stories function to bring God's presence into our lives. The gospel in story is a happening-reality. The story works by involving people in its reality. We must simply let the story do its work![15]

In appendix I of this book, I have included a list of additional resources that help frame the Bible as a narrative.

THE WIKISTORY

Coming to the Bible as a story helps us to get a sense of its interconnected narrative, a winding epic that is not-so-neatly joined together through plots and characters. Author and artist Colin Harbinson describes the value of seeing the Bible's storyline this way:

> The Bible is not a mere jumble of history, poetry, lessons in morality and theology, comforting promises, guiding principles and commands; instead, it is fundamentally coherent. Every part of the Bible—each event, book, character, command, prophecy, and poem—must be understood in the context of one storyline.
>
> Many of us have read the Bible as if it were merely a mosaic of little bits—theological bits, moral bits, historical-critical bits, sermon bits, devotional bits. But when we read the Bible in such a fragmented way, we ignore its divine author's intention to shape our lives through its story.
>
> All human communities live out some story that provides a

context for understanding the meaning of history, and that gives shape and direction to their lives. If we allow the Bible to become fragmented, it is in danger of being absorbed into whatever other story is shaping our culture, and it will thus cease to shape our lives as it should.[16]

It would be nice if the Bible read like a novel from cover to cover. But it's not a novel. It's a series of books that have been grouped together—and many of them are out of chronological order.

In technological terminology, a mashup is a Web application that combines data from more than one source into a single integrated tool. The Bible is like this—a mashup of different writings from different authors inspired to tell a unified story about God and God's actions in the world.

Author Scot McKnight suggests we look at the Bible as a "Wikistory," in which there is "ongoing reworking of the biblical story by new authors who each tell the story in their own way." McKnight continued, "None [of the books of the Bible] is exhaustive, comprehensive or absolute . . . they are different stories of the Story. We don't have to harmonize them or try to reconcile them. They're just doing their own versions of the Story, and each has a place in the larger picture."[17]

Let's face it—the Bible is often difficult to read and to teach. We've got our work cut out for us if we wish to provide a sense of its overarching story. That's why Bible storying is the best way I've found to give people, young and old alike, a Bible overview with context to all future Bible learning.

A KINGDOM THREAD

When I began to get a sense of the entire narrative and see the Bible as one story, a common thread came into focus for me—a helpful storyline that runs through the entirety of Scripture. While many themes and symbols can be found repeated throughout Scripture, none seems more predominant than the kingdom of God.

My pastor, Joel Kline of Highland Avenue Church of the Brethren in

Elgin, Illinois, recently described the biblical story as "the alternative story of life in the kingdom of God—an invitation to live, here and now, as if God's kingdom were fully present among us. It is a call to embrace Christ's new story for our living, a story that speaks of new possibilities in God's kingdom—a realm of living based not on oppressive control and domination over others, but on bottom-up service; a realm of living marked not by a clenched fist but by open, wounded hands extended in a welcoming embrace of kindness, gentleness, forgiveness, and grace. . . a realm of living ever seeking to expand the circles of God's renewing love."

From the very beginnings of the story, God expresses a desire to live in close harmony with creation and for creation to enjoy God's kingdom. God created humans as image-bearers of the divine, continuing God's creativity and care of creation on earth. But humans decided to create their own kingdoms, where they could live according to their own desires.

So God set in motion a kingdom agenda to restore creation to wholeness. Story after Bible story describes the amazing lengths God went to in order to extend grace to us—to give humans opportunities to repair our broken relationship with God. God even came and dwelled with the Jewish nation—a community chosen to live distinctly reflecting the ways of God the King.

The apex of the kingdom storyline is found in Jesus. Jesus announced the kingdom of God breaking into history, displaying God's restorative power in his life, miracles, and words. At the cross, Jesus gained decisive victory over evil and empire for us, liberating us from the power of sin. Then Jesus entered as the firstborn into the resurrection life of restored creation. God's Spirit was sent to continue the restorative work, empowering a global community of people called the church to embody God's kingdom and join in God's actions in the world."

RECLAIMING OUR ROLES AS STORYTELLERS

In light of our history and current culture, we have a responsibility to reevaluate our methods of communicating the Bible. I believe that in order to be effective, we must reclaim our roles as storytellers, embracing them in the form of artful narrators and prophetic historians.

Artful Narrators

Storytelling is more like the work of an artist than a teacher. It's less about explaining what something means and more about allowing others to explore the meaning for themselves. The hope is that listeners will make their own connections between the Story and their own stories, as this has a much greater impact than any connections we might try to make for them. This is different from preaching or teaching in that we're not in total control of the conclusions that others may draw from what we say.

Here are some excerpts that speak to the idea of artful narration.

> As the biblical story unfolds, it does so in stories and poetry. In fact, approximately 75 percent of scripture consists of narrative, 15 percent is expressed in poetic forms, and only 10 percent is propositional and overtly instructional in nature. In our retelling of the same story, we have reversed this biblical pattern. Today an estimated ten percent of our communication is designed to capture the imagination of the listener, while 90 percent is purely instructive.[18]
> —COLIN HARBINSON

> Our literate tradition trained us to find the ideas in the Bible and shape them in logical ways for the preaching task. . . we have learned how to use Scripture as the source of ideas we wish to inculcate in the life of our people. There is another possibility. We can also fill their heads with people! We can tell biblical stories in such a way that the characters of the Bible come to live in the hearts and minds of our listeners. . . One of the ways in which Christ can be formed within us is the way of biblical characters living within our consciousness.[19] —RICHARD JENSEN

> The new conversations, on which our very lives depend, require a poet, not a moralist. Because finally church people are like other people; we are not changed by new rules. The deep places in our lives—places of resistance and embrace—are not ultimately reached by instruction. Those places of

resistance and embrace are reached only by stories, by images, metaphors and phrases that line out the world differently, apart from fear or hurt.[20] —WALTER BRUEGGEMANN

Prophetic Historians

Is there a place for the teacher and the expert in church today? Yes, I believe there is. I believe those with the gift of teaching need to major in the art of facilitating discussion (more on that in coming chapters), become artful narrators, and reframe their roles as prophetic historians.

Prophetic what. . . ? Teachers should invest themselves deeply in the study of the ancient cultures of the Bible, so they can bring that world to life in their communities of faith. Prophetic historians give us real insights into the text and help us to enter the world of the stories we find there. Bible scholar Kenton Sparks encourages us that in order to "get the sense of the discourse, we must imagine a context, in terms of the thoughts and intentions of authors and audiences, that will make the written text sensible."[21]

Pastor David Fitch describes the new role of preaching this way: "Instead of dissecting the text, making it portable, and distributing it to people for their own personal use, the preacher re-narrates the world as it is under the Lordship of Christ and then invites people into it."[22] Prophetic historians have unique gifts of helping us experience the past and connecting their messages to a bigger Story. They are always mindful to place their present content in the context of the broader story of the Bible.

New Testament scholar Marcus Borg points to the importance of reinvigorating an understanding of the ancient cultures in the Bible:

> To be Christian means to live within the world created by the Bible. We are to listen to it well and let its central stories shape our vision of God, our identity, and our sense of what faithfulness to God means. It is to shape our imagination, that part of our psyches in which our foundational images of reality and life reside. We are to be a community shaped by scripture. The purpose of our continuing dialogue with the Bible as sacred scripture is nothing less than that.[23]

QUESTIONS FOR REFLECTION AND DISCUSSION

> *Which parts of this chapter did you relate to your own story?*

> *What "stories" do you see the people around you giving their lives to?*

> *What areas of life have you seen the story of consumerism permeate?*

> *What approaches to reading the Bible have you experienced?*

> *How might stories reshape the way you teach and learn from the Bible?*

A TRUE STORY ABOUT STORYING

This past year, our youth ministry spent twenty-two weeks making our way through the story of God. Each episode brought to life stories that my students had heard since they were kids but had never seen as being applicable to their lives.

When we first began, the main comment the leaders heard was, "We've heard these stories before." But as the students wrestled with the stories, they soon realized they didn't know the stories as well as they thought they did. They found a freedom to ask questions they'd always been too afraid to ask in Sunday school, fearing they'd stump the teacher.

God did some amazing things in those weeks. Two students came to know Christ as a result of the story of God. We also had many new believers who couldn't get enough. Students who'd been Christians for years were being challenged in new ways and by stories they'd heard for years.

As a result, the students in our ministry have really taken ownership of God's story. They now see the big picture of how God demonstrated his love for mankind and restored our relationship to him. My students also understand that they're a continuation of that story. On the last night, we had an empty canvas displayed at the front of the room. I challenged the students to come up and write about how they'd continue the story. Their comments were amazing, and that canvas now hangs in our youth room as a reminder of our commitment.

The story of God has made a profound impact on my ministry. It's laid a foundation that I can now build on. It's so encouraging to see how the students are now able to fit our weekly lessons into the big picture of God's story.

—**DAVE LANE**, YOUTH WORKER IN SARNIA, ONTARIO

CHAPTER EIGHT

TURNING THE DIAMOND

> Narratives by their very nature are multivalent; they have many meanings that touch different levels of out lives and address the different issues brought by the hearer of the story. Too often religions communities assign one meaning or moral to the story and close out other, deeper, truer possibilities.[1]
>
> — H. STEPHEN SHOEMAKER,
>   *GODSTORIES: NEW NARRATIVES FROM SACRED TEXTS*

THE ORAL TRADITION

The Ancient Israelites and the Early Christians were storytelling cultures. It's widely accepted that most of the Hebrew (Old Testament) Scriptures first existed as oral stories for generations (some for centuries) before they were committed to written form. The Exile of the Kingdoms of Judah and Israel prompted great concern that the stories of their faith would be lost, so it was around the time of these events that a great many of the biblical accounts were recorded in order to be preserved. Preceding—and alongside—the written Torah was an "oral Torah" also known as the oral tradition.

Ancient Jewish people knew the Scriptures very well from telling and retelling stories of their faith. Listeners of the Torah were required to retell it the way they'd been taught. The early church also followed this practice, with families passing down stories of faith to each generation.[2]

Storytelling was a vital part of the fabric of the Ancient Jewish culture. They didn't use a phonetic alphabet, and the Hebrew language only contains a fraction of the number of words found in Greek and English. So each word in Hebrew serves multiple meanings, making the verbal and physical expression of those words vital to interpret their meaning.

As part of their storytelling identity, centuries ago Jewish teachers developed midrash—stories told by rabbinic teachers providing commentary on the Hebrew Scriptures. Midrash "fills in the cracks . . . puts flesh on the bones . . . reinterprets stories and characters . . . gives a voice to those in the story who have no voice."[3] This ancient practice continues today, exhibiting the remarkable imagination and storytelling ability of the Jewish people, as they add character and texture to biblical accounts.

Well beyond the time of Jesus, the primary experience of scripture continued to be storytelling. Jesus was known as a powerful storyteller, as described in Mark 4:33-34 (The Message): "With many stories like these, [Jesus] presented his message to them, fitting the stories to their experience and maturity. He was never without a story when he spoke. When he was alone with his disciples, he went over everything, sorting out the tangles, untying the knots."

In fact, the Bible tells us that "Jesus spoke all these things to the crowd in parables; he did not say anything to them without using a parable" (Matthew 13:34 NLT). Parables are stories that draw a parallel to our lives. Jesus used parables to describe life around him, using everyday objects to teach deep truths. He related to a society of farmers and fishermen with stories that were interesting, easy to remember, and life changing. Jesus saw the value of helping others see the big picture of Scripture from the beginning. He related his story to his culture within the context of the grand story.

One of my favorite references to storytelling in the New Testament is when Jesus was walking on the road to Emmaus shortly after his resurrection (quoted here from Luke 24:27,32, NIV): "And beginning with Moses and all the Prophets, [Jesus] explained to them what was said in all the Scriptures concerning himself. . . . They asked each other, 'Were not our hearts burning within us while he talked with us on the road and opened the Scriptures to us?'"

Jesus was telling them *the* story, starting way back with Moses, and connecting the story all the way to their present lives. Jesus knew the power of the Scriptures and used it to help his disciples find themselves in that story.

The Bible isn't just full of stories; it's also full of storytellers: Moses (Exodus), David (Psalms 78, 105, 106), Nehemiah (Nehemiah 9), Stephen (Acts 7), and Paul (Acts 13, Galatians 3 and 4), just to name a few. These believers inspired and challenged people with true accounts of God's activity and faithfulness.

It seems that when a culture comes to the Scriptures in an oral rather than written form, it causes them to treat the Scriptures in a different way. The Hebrew culture looked at the Scriptures as stories to live by, carrying the Scriptures in their minds and hearts, listening intently to experience the stories, allowing them to teach, shape, and unify their society.

> The Hebrew culture looked at the Scriptures as stories to live by, carrying the Scriptures in their minds and hearts, listening intently to experience the stories, allowing them to teach, shape, and unify their society.

My hope is that we, as followers of Jesus, will begin to regain the beauty and richness of the storytelling tradition that's a part of Christian heritage.

THE SEVENTY FACES OF TORAH

The Jewish tradition possesses a unique reverence for the Scriptures. For thousands of years they have been encouraged to regard the Scriptures as a "living person"—with respect and complexity—and take the time to get to know her.[4] Some rabbis have described this relationship as a dance, where the Scripture is given the lead, and the community does its best not to step on her toes! In ancient times, interaction with the Torah was always done in a group, as they invited the Scriptures to be a key part of the community's dialogue.

For centuries, Jews have been invited to actively search out "multiple layers of meaning" in the Scriptures. According to the ancient Jewish perspective, approaching the text with a belief that there is just one meaning or purpose would be gravely underestimating the power of the Scriptures. Jewish tradition teaches that their are four dynamics of meaning in every verse of Scripture:

> P'shat —The plain (historical/grammatical) meaning.

> Remez —The meaning that is only hinted at.

> Derash —The implicit meaning.

> Sod —The mystery and esoteric meaning.[5]

This framework does not suggest only four possible outcomes. In the Jewish mind, the potential to derive meaning from the Scripture is endless. Author H. Stephen Shoemaker describes this perspective in his book *Godstories: New Narratives from Sacred Texts*:

> Rabbinic tradition says there are at least seventy facets to each word of scripture . . . there is a "divine valence," or divine intention underlying every text. But we cannot completely grasp that with our infinite minds. Therefore, we search out the meaning of the text in order to draw closer to the divine meaning–freed from the constraints of trying of finding one "correct" meaning. Narratives by their very nature are multivalent; they have many meanings that touch different levels of our lives and address the different issues brought by the hearer of the story. Too often religions communities assign one meaning or moral to the story and close out other, deeper, truer possibilities.[6]

For nearly a thousand years, Jewish rabbis have passed on a metaphor to explain this special multivalent perspective of Scripture. They call it the Seventy Faces of Torah, as they compare Scripture to a beautiful diamond with seventy sides or faces, which they should turn "around and around, for everything is in it."[7] Stephen M. Wylen describes this metaphor in detail in his book *The Seventy Faces of Torah*:

> Shiv'im panim laTorah—"There are seventy faces to the Torah." Every single verse in the Torah yields seventy different interpretations. Each interpretation teaches

something new and different. They may even contradict one another. . . . Yet each one of the seventy interpretations is the true word of God.

The image of the seventy faces may be taken from the imagery of the jeweler's art. Each side of a cut gem is called a facet, a little face. A light sparkles within every fine gemstone. We know that this light is a reflection, but the ancients thought of the light in a gemstone as originating from within the stone. The beauty and fascination of a fine gem is that one stone sparkles in so many different ways. We know there is a single light within the stone, but we see that light differently depending on which face we gaze upon. One diamond is like seventy different diamonds as we turn it, but of course it is one. In the same way there is only one God, whose light shines forth from every verse in the Torah. We see that light differently depending on how we interpret the verse. The unitary light of God's Holy Spirit is fully revealed in many sparkles and flashes, as we seek God through a multitude of interpretations on every single verse of Scripture.[8]

As the ancient Jewish people listened and looked deeply into the Torah, they anticipated that each person would see something unique reflected back——further detail, beauty, depth, and brilliance—illuminated from the same source of light, God's Spirit.

As they gathered to listen and look attentively into the Scriptures, they'd engage in lively dialogue, sharing all that they'd seen reflected back to them in the Seventy Faces of Torah. Though they were familiar with these stories, an attitude of expectancy and wonder prevailed; they would say, "We know these stories, but we do not yet know them." These were spirited discussions, sometimes turning toward disagreement, with shouting and laughter being commonplace.[9] Many Jews carry on this tradition with the belief that God continues to reveal more of Godself each time they gather and learn from the Scriptures.

We too, should embrace this approach to the Scriptures. The Bible and its stories are living, filled with endless meaning and mystery that we can connect with today. Each reflection shows us something new. We must listen as God's Spirit illuminates the Scriptures for us—turning the diamond—allowing our imaginations to explore them and the implications of the story to settle on us.

Bible storying helps create this kind of environment, one in which God's Spirit can speak through the imaginations of the community, encouraging a broad range of voices to share what God is illuminating to them in that moment.

STORY, IMAGINATION, AND FAITH

Exploring the multivalence of scripture requires thoughtful, imaginative observation that moves us to make meaning.

Imagination seems to open the doorway to another dimension. It allows us to explore another part of who we are—a part of us where our faith lies. Could it be that faith is an imaginative process? I've often wondered if we can fully embrace a spiritual truth without it being processed by our imaginations. It seems that we must creatively form ideas and images in our minds to give meaning to them. I don't mean to say that faith is imaginary. On the contrary, it brings to reality that which is not present to our senses.

Author and theologian C. S. Lewis writes, "For me, reason is the natural organ of truth; but imagination is the organ of meaning. Imagination, producing new metaphors or revivifying old, is not the cause of truth, but its condition."[10] We might think that imagination is just something to help us escape reality, but this quote suggests it's much more. Imagination opens up new ways of thinking—it activates our senses and feelings. But imagination also takes us deeper: I believe that God uses our imaginations to help us find meaning.

Sarah Arthur, in her book *The God-Hungry Imagination*, writes, "Imagination gives us the ability to find and make purposeful patterns and even plot-lines: in other words, the ability to find and make meaning." She continues, "Imagination is how we put things together. It's how we make connections between thought and experience, word and image, self and other, seen and unseen."[11]

I believe that imagination can fuel the transformation process. It's the key to processing the abstract and building faith. Imagination helps us weave an interior pattern that makes sense of life. And in order to create the best environments for transformation, we must take every opportunity to cultivate imagination in our ministries.

Bible storying aims to empower our imaginations and transport us into the world of the Bible. Bible stories are embedded in an ancient culture that we must creatively work to understand in order to participate in the story. As the Israelites retold their sacred stories over and over, they invited each other to *zah-kor*. This is a Hebrew word that means to remember. But this word means much more than just recalling something from the past; it suggests active engagement—reliving and participating again. When the Israelites listened to the stories of their faith, they put themselves in the story alongside their ancestors.

> **Imagination helps us weave an interior pattern that makes sense of life.**

Entering the Bible imaginatively is not a suggestion to check our brains at the door. On the contrary, I'm suggesting we think more deeply—using our intuition, critical thinking skills, creativity, and rational minds —all in harmony to make meaningful connections.

Approaching the Bible through a narrative lens opens up a gateway to imagination and meaning. In his book *Experiential Storytelling*, Mark Miller writes:

> Storytelling is powerful because it has the ability to touch human beings at the most personal level. While facts are viewed from the lens of a microscope, stories are viewed from the lens of the soul. Stories address us on every level. They speak to the mind, the body, the emotions, the spirit, and the will. In a story a person can identify with situations he or she has never been in. The individual's imagination is unlocked to dream what was previously unimaginable.[12]

Story unleashes the part of us that processes meaning and the abstract, metaphors and analogies, helping us as we try to grasp the invisible and indefinable. Story helps us go beyond learning that's simply knowledge to learning that's embodied.

QUESTIONS FOR REFLECTION AND DISCUSSION

› *What resonated with you from this chapter?*

› *How might ancient Jewish perspectives on the Scriptures inform us today?*

› *How have you found scripture to be multivalent?*

› *How might imagination be "the organ of meaning"?*

› *How might imagination be important to faith?*

A TRUE STORY ABOUT STORYING

First, it is a bit unnerving to lead something and trust that the Holy Spirit will come through! But, once I was able to "let go and let God," I felt relaxed and ready. There were a couple times I wanted to jump in and "explain" something about the creation story (specifically the piece about being made in God's image), but it was a young adult who piped up and shared a different perspective. That's what I love about this. People may come away with different viewpoints on the story—*but*, we all hear the "wondering" without judgment, and all the wondering helps us to see things in a new light.

I began by explaining the seventy Faces of Torah (to me, that is a helpful image) and I think it was important to stress the "expectation" piece of that...that as we study scripture, we can expect God to show us something and *everyone* has something to contribute. No one person can claim they have all the answers. People were hesitant to share their pictures/poems, but I don't think that mattered, because what *did* happen was that everyone felt comfortable sharing their wondering questions and observations. *I love it!*

I asked folks to write down their comments and a few people responded:

› This was helpful. It engaged everyone and gave us all a new vision for how to listen to Bible stories and participate in conversation about them.

› I want to cover more of the Bible like this!

› Loved this type of "lesson." I would like to do more.

› It was really cool to experience a different way of Bible studying (from a youth in the group).

—KAREN MATTHIAS-LONG, DENOMINATIONAL STAFF LEADER, NORTHEAST PENNSYLVANIA

CHAPTER NINE

STORYING & LEARNING

Tell me and I will forget.
Show me, and I may remember.
Involve me, and I will understand.
—CONFUCIUS, 450 BC

A visit to my wife's school and elementary classroom was eye-opening. Right away, I noticed a significant focus on multiple learning modes. Classrooms were arranged with designated areas to accommodate learning through sight, sound, and touch. Every subject's curriculum was adapted to meet the needs of left- and right-brain processing, including tools for multisensory teaching.

I thought, "this is different than when I was in school." As my wife and I dialogued about this, she shared how there was strong research and proven educational theory behind the structure of their classrooms and curricula.

I immediately began researching and experimenting with new ways of teaching and learning. I saw students come alive in their faith and participate more fully that I had ever before. As I did so, it felt as though I was entering a whole new world—one left largely unexplored by the church. I was deeply compelled to learn more and be better equipped for creating experiential learning opportunities. So I pursued a master of education in integrated learning (the study of how people best learn). This pursuit has grown into a lifelong passion to help churches explore the intersection of spiritual formation and experiential learning.

In my studies, I found two approaches to identifying the ways in which we learn:

> Types of Learners: How we interact with information

> Types of Thinkers: How we process information

TYPES OF LEARNERS

We receive information through our senses and, generally, the more senses we involve in any learning experience, the better we'll retain the information. However, each of us has a proclivity toward certain sensory learning modes. If we're not given the opportunity to use those senses, then we tend to switch off and are far less likely to learn effectively.

Most of us are predominantly one type of learner, but depending on the environment, we may adapt to other types. These are most common types of learners:

Visual Learners

> Connect best with information by watching

> Identify images to relate to an experience

> Respond well to images, graphics, symbols, diagrams, and demonstrations

Literary Learners

> Connect best with information by reading

> Identify words to relate to an experience

> Respond well to printed words, concepts, and through writing

Auditory Learners

> Connect best with information by hearing

> Identify sounds to relate to an experience

> Respond well to spoken words, dialogue, music, and poems

Hands-on (Kinesthetic) Learners

> Connect best with information by touch and movement

> Identify feelings to relate to an experience

> Respond well to drawing, object lessons, field trips, and participation

Which type of learner are you? In my experiential learning workshops I take an informal poll on which one of these types best describe the way they learn. While I have not documented the results, I continue to notice a growing number of people indicating that they are hands-on learners. This makes me wonder what effect technology might have on shaping the way people learn. People (especially youth and children) are accustomed to interacting with information and entertainment in visual and physical ways. Through the Internet they can pull up facts, video, and images about most anything. Then they can reshape it, mix it up, and recreate it as their own. Teens don't just watch videos on YouTube anymore. They remake them as a creative response. Technology is contributing to our impatience with one-directional communication. The new norm for adolescents is creating while they learn.

> **The new norm for adolescents is creating while they learn.**

TYPES OF THINKERS

Thinking type differs from learning type in that it has more to do with how we cognitively process information than how our senses interact with it. As with learning types, most people are predisposed (but not limited) to one of these types, but some people function well using two or three types.

Education experts Peter Honey and Alan Mumford identified four different types of thinkers: reflective (analytic), creative (active), practical (pragmatic), and conceptual (theorist).[1] I've adapted the descriptions of these types to bring some additional clarity and usefulness.

Reflective (Analytic) Thinkers

> Analytical and careful
> Prefer to keep a low profile
> View new information subjectively
> Take time to ponder and make observations
> Relate new information to past experiences
> Examine their feelings about what they're learning
> Don't like to be rushed to make quick decisions

Practical (Pragmatic) Thinkers

> Seek the simplest, most efficient way
> Prefer to act quickly and get impatient with process
> Desire immediate relevance
> Not satisfied without specific applications and directions
> Want factual information
> Accept new information only after seeing the big picture

Creative (Active) Thinkers

> Imaginative, enthusiastic, and open-ended
> Prefer activity and attention
> Make excellent troubleshooters
> Create their own solutions and shortcuts
> Tend to get bored easily, dislike repetition
> Learn well from reading and synthesizing information

Conceptual (Theorist) Thinkers

> Value rationality and logic above all
> Prefer to analyze and synthesize
> Want to know how things work and learn related concepts
> Can be detached from their emotions
> Uncomfortable with subjectivity and ambiguity
> Like to be intellectually stretched

LEARNING CONNECTIONS

As we explore types of learning and thought, we can only assume that we—and our students—will connect better and assume a more active role at different segments of the storying process. I'm a visual / kinesthetic learner, so I was concerned that storying wouldn't connect with my need to "see it." However, I learned that stories have the ability to draw in any learning type because of their imaginative nature.

Storying is a perfect tool for meeting the needs of different types of learners. It involves participants right from the start and through a variety of learning methods: storytelling, visualizing, dialogue, reflection, creative activities—you name it. (For a more detailed description of each of the parts of the Bible storying process, see chapter 11).

STORYING PART	LEARNING CONNECTION
REWIND Connect with story symbols to review previous stories	› **Visual Learners—connects with symbols their "mental timeline"** › Auditory Learners—rehearing past stories / verbal processing › Hands-on Learners—like re-enactments and drawing of the symbols › Literary Learners—like the chronology of stories
	› Reflective Thinkers—like to relate information to past experiences › Creative Thinkers—like creative and imaginative dynamics › **Practical Thinkers—get to replay facts of previous stories** › Conceptual Thinkers—see how stories interrelate

*BOLD indicates whom it connects the best with

STORYING PART	LEARNING CONNECTION
PREPARE Focus our minds for imaginative listening	› Visual Learners—visualize framing metaphor
	› **Auditory Learners—like listening to framing metaphor**
	› Physical Learners—like breathing exercise, focusing attention
	› Literary Learners—like having a place to write
	› **Reflective Thinkers—like to slow down and focus their mind**
	› Creative Thinkers—like to anticipate the story about to be told
	› Practical Thinkers—appreciate knowing what is expected of them
	› Conceptual Thinkers—love metaphors

STORYING PART	LEARNING CONNECTION
IMAGINE Listen actively to a live telling of a Bible story	› Visual Learners—vivid descriptions spark mental imagery
	› **Auditory Learners—vivid audible descriptions**
	› Hands-on Learners—draw or take notes to follow along
	› Literary Learners—connect with specific words and phrases
	› Reflective Thinkers—connect with emotion of story, good listeners
	› **Creative Thinkers—like creative and imaginative language**
	› Practical Thinkers—emphasis on small details
	› Conceptual Thinkers—emphasis on big picture and ideas

STORYING PART	LEARNING CONNECTION
CAPTURE Record observations by sketching or writing	› Visual Learners—drawing and artistic mediums › Auditory Learners—processing thoughts on paper and verbal sharing › **Hands-on Learners—artistic mediums and participation** › Literary Learners—like being able to write thoughts and concepts
	› Reflective Thinkers—like quiet to be able to process › Creative Thinkers—like options to express themselves › Practical Thinkers—capture concrete events from the story › **Conceptual Thinkers—name big ideas from the story**

STORYING PART	LEARNING CONNECTION
REMIX* Choose from drawing or writing activities to retell part of story in your own way *THIS PART OF THE PROCESS IS ADDED IN THE ECHO THE STORY CURRICULUM AND NOT A PART OF THE MY BASIC BIBLE STORYING PROCESS.	› Visual Learners—like artistic mediums › Auditory Learners—get to processing thoughts out loud › **Hand-on Learners— like artistic mediums and participation** › Literary Learners—like being able to read and respond to printed scripture
	› Reflective Thinkers—focus on the characters and emotion of the story › Creative Thinkers—like creative and imaginative expression › **Practical Thinkers—like guidance through a specific activity** › Conceptual Thinkers—get to synthesize their ideas about the story

STORYING PART	LEARNING CONNECTION
CONNECT Share insights through guided dialogue	› Visual Learners—like imaginative questions that draw out imagery › **Auditory Learners—sharing and listening to observations** › Hands-on Learners—participation in a discussion › Literary Learners—capture others words and concepts
	› Reflective Thinkers—create a safe place to process information › Creative Thinkers—enjoy imaginative questions and diversity of ideas › **Practical Thinkers—make real-life connections** › Conceptual Thinkers—can share theories and synthesis of story

STORYING FOLLOWS THE EXPERIENTIAL LEARNING CYCLE

Learning is rooted in experiencing the information, not the information itself. Education pioneer John Dewey said, "there is an intimate and necessary relation between the processes of actual experience and education."[2] Dewey's writing and educational philosophy is the basis of many Western theories of education and largely shaped the Experiential Learning Cycle.

> Learning is rooted in experiencing the information, not the information itself.

Developed by educational expert David Kolb in 1984, the Experiential Learning Cycle (sometimes called the Applied Learning Cycle) is based on decades of research about how the integration of learning works. Kolb's Cycle is the most widely used and accepted model in education describing the sequence and application of learning. Kolb said, "Learning is the process whereby knowledge is created through the transformation of experience."[3] The heart of Kolb's model proposes four stages that move us toward applied learning: Experience, Reflect, Interpret and Plan.

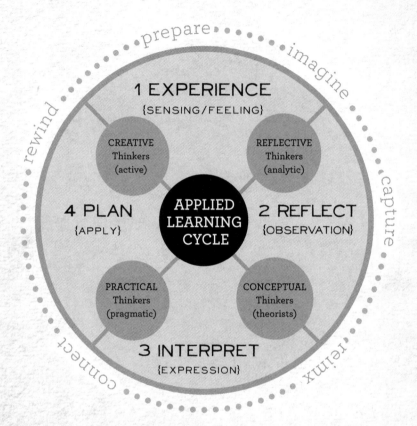

You may also notice that it connects with all four types of thinkers at different points in the continuum. I've adapted the wording and descriptions of these stages to offer some additional clarity and usefulness. I've also overlaid the segments of Bible storying onto the diagram so you can see how it follows the Experiential Learning Cycle.

Kolb's model isn't just informative; it's also a helpful tool for evaluation. We can examine our ministries in light of this cycle, assessing whether we're balanced in providing learning opportunities at each stage. Investing in each stage of the cycle is critical, as the stages are interdependent and build upon each other. And each stage contributes to forming a foundation for subsequent learning.

For example, one youth worker's Tuesday-night small group regularly skims over the Reflect and Interpret stages, spending little time looking in depth at background and context of the Bible passage being studied. The leader says, "We like to get right to the application and answer the question, 'What does this mean for us?'" As a result, the group seems impatient with background information and struggles to value the Bible's context. (I've been there!) This Bible study contributes to its members' lack of foundation for learning based on the Scriptures. This seems to be a big problem in many churches in America.

It's important for us to follow the entire cycle in order to facilitate effective learning. Students who experience this process on a regular basis will appreciate the opportunity to engage in ways that fit them, to build self-confidence, to share more frequently, and will be more open to try new things.

As teachers, we gravitate toward particular segments of the learning cycle. I know I could spend all day in the Interpret segment—I love asking questions and letting ideas circulate! The danger in doing this is if time is short, then we'll tend to focus only on our favorite parts of the cycle, cutting short the rest. If we don't want to exclude some of our students from developing to their full potential, then we must practice giving equal weight to every part of the cycle.

The great thing is that the process of Bible storying works well within the Experiential Learning Cycle. Storying calls us to facilitate an experience of the Bible that helps participants develop as learners, growing their skills to discover and create as an act of worship to God.

The purpose of the Experiential Learning Cycle is to move participants to "applied learning" (in other words, learning that invokes changes in thought and behavior). Educators use the term development to describe these changes, while we in the church use the term *formation*. In this context, both terms describe the same idea—*internal shaping and growth that leads toward outward action*.

Discipleship involves more than a transfer of information (informative); it's a relationship that involves being shaped by

God, God's story, and others' stories—it is formation (formative). Experiencing the Bible as story is a catalyst for formation. I believe God inhabits the biblical story, illuminating it to us, drawing us into it, and reshaping our perspective. Through the Story, God gives us new eyes, and the Story begins to permeate and reorder all areas of our lives.

Preben Vang and Terry Carter describe the transformative power of God's Story in their book *Telling God's Story:*

> Our lives as human beings are made up of stories that have shaped, or are shaping, who we are. The story of the Bible has the power to make sense of all the other stories of your life. When it is internalized and it becomes your story, it gives meaning in the midst of meaninglessness and value in the midst of worthlessness. Your personal story will find grounding in creation, guidance in crises, re-formation in redemption, and direction in its destination. People become Christians when their own stories merge with, and are understood in the light of, God's story.[4]

A LEARNER-CENTERED FOCUS

As we begin to study the most effective methods of helping others learn, we discover that moving from teacher/lecture-based to learner-based methods is imperative. Years of research have shown that motivation, learning, and success are enhanced when learner-centered principles and practices are in place. Throughout North America, educational institutions on all levels have transitioned to a learner-centered philosophy of teaching.

Storying is designed as learner-centered teaching. To effectively lead the storying process will require all of us to adopt new methods, to let go of some of the control we're used to having, to seek patience, and to trust the Holy Spirit to speak to and through a community of learners.

Maryellen Weimer, author of *Learner-Centered Teaching*, says that in order for teaching to promote learning more effectively, our thinking and practices need to change in five areas:

1. **The Role of the Teacher**
   We move into a role of coaching and mentoring students to facilitate their own learning, designing experiences through which students acquire new knowledge and develop new skills. The goal of all teachers should be enabling students to be lifelong learners, and giving them tools to succeed in this venture.

2. **The Balance of Power**
   The effectiveness of learner-centered methods depends on teachers being able to step aside and let students take the lead. However, having been at the center for so long, we may find it tough to leave that spot, even briefly.

3. **The Function of Content**
   The underlying philosophy is that students learn best not only by receiving knowledge, but also by interpreting it, learning through discovery, and setting the pace for their own learning.

4. **The Responsibility for Learning**
   We need to shift responsibility for learning to the students. The primary goal of a teacher is to create a "climate for learning." Don't underestimate your power to model a passion for learning.

5. **The Purpose and Processes of Evaluation**
   In this model, evaluation and purposes shift. It becomes less about students taking away our specific applications and more about a myriad of implications as they involve themselves in teaching and learning from each other. This method of learning is messy—a lot more like real life![5]

BECOME AN EXPERIENCE ARCHITECT

One of the defining words for this digital era is *interactive*. We're becoming accustomed to being able to access and create our own media at a moment's notice. We desire to contribute to our own learning and formation like we would any conversation. We now yearn to be a part of a shared experience.

This shift in values has significant implications for the way we approach education. Places where we've traditionally accessed information—schools, libraries, and museums—have identified this shift and moved to making their learning opportunities more interactive. There is a new set of standards for how we teach others. We are moving away from one-dimensional education with the teachers being the experts who hold the key to information.

> We desire to contribute to our own learning and formation like we would any conversation. We now yearn to be a part of a shared experience.

Students already have instant access to most information. They're becoming accustomed to being able to change, interact, and create while they learn.

We teachers and leaders then become guides to help students explore information and use it in the right context. This requires a new vision for our roles as educators. We become "experience architects," creating environments that help participants dive deeper and explore further in their experience of God. This new role requires a significant investment of energy into creativity.

Storying will help you explore your new role as an experience architect. The storying process encourages you to experiment with all kinds of creative exercises that will foster learning and formation in your group.

QUESTIONS FOR REFLECTION AND DISCUSSION

> *What type of learner are you? What type of thinker are you?*

> *What learning environments and methods have you connected with the best?*

> *What part of the Experiential Learning Cycle energizes you? What part is most challenging for you to engage with?*

> *Do you believe it's important for ministries to embrace learner-centered methods? Why?*

> *What are some ways you could make your ministry more learner-centered?*

A TRUE STORY ABOUT STORYING

I grew up cultured in story. From movies to my friends' fables of their past experiences, I was consumed with a narrative. But it took a little while to figure out that stories are a large part of Scripture. I interned under Michael Novelli for my undergraduate work in youth ministry. He loved this "new" concept and talked about how it adds so much depth to our understanding of the Scriptures, as well as our relationship to them. I slowly caught on, and I, too, have seen the impact of storying, both personally and in my ministry.

The year following my time with Michael, my friend Joe and I were asked to start up a youth program for a local church. As Joe and I discussed our thoughts and convictions about what this new ministry could be, I was quick to suggest the element of storying. So for the first year, Joe and I tried to build relationships with the students. And during our Sunday evening gatherings, we'd come together for a story. It started slowly—the concept seemed elementary to most of the students (and parents and volunteers). Joe and I, however, stuck it out; and since then, we've begun to see something beautiful emerge.

My students who had little to no Bible knowledge were starting to get it; they began entering into and making connections with the stories to see the redemptive rainbow that unites the Scriptures.

Seeing Scripture as God's story became an annual rhythm of our year. The students started creating art and relating it to Scripture. Each week would be something different. For instance, when we participated in the story of creation, the students had to create with clay something that represented the human condition. Most of them created something that represented the idea of wholeness, connectedness with the Godhead, happiness. When we went into the rebellion of mankind, they were asked to create something that represented the state of humanity with sin in the picture. In the youth room, we maintained an open wall for student art—a place to display the students' masterpieces about the stories.

Storying helped our students become more knowledgeable about Scripture and its narrative of redemption and restoration. It also gave them a more complete view of the Bible.

—**CHRIS STEWART**, YOUTH WORKER IN ELGIN, ILLINOIS

PART THREE
how to lead Bible storying

CHAPTER TEN

DEVELOPING BIBLE STORYING

Bible storying is an imaginative way to experience the Bible using storytelling, creative reflection, and dialogue. This approach helps participants discover meaning and identity in the biblical narrative.

THE BIBLE STORYING MOVEMENT

My approach to this method, as described in this book, was originally derived from my experiences and training in chronological Bible storying. Missionaries who felt that understanding and remembering the gospel should not hinge on literacy introduced chronological Bible storying (CBS) a few decades ago. CBS has become a worldwide movement, led in partnership between Campus Crusade for Christ, the International Mission Board of the Southern Baptist Convention, Trans World Radio, Wycliffe International, YWAM, and many more organizations, churches, and individuals. A key communication hub for this movement is the website www.oralitystrategies.org.

> Bible storying is an imaginative way to experience the Bible using storytelling, creative reflection, and dialogue.

Leaders of this movement describe Chronological Bible storying this way: "CBS is the process of encountering God by telling the stories of the Bible. In CBS, we tell Bible stories without interruption or comment and we tell them in the order that they happened in time. Afterward, we discuss each story and its significance for our lives. Each story builds on those that came before; as a result, the overarching message of the Bible becomes clear and we discover our own place in God's story."[1]

While my approach to Bible storying certainly falls within this definition, I continue to evolve and adapt it for varying contexts.

I have changed my approach and process over the years (and from the first printing of this book) based on firsthand experiences and experiments and a desire to incorporate more experiential learning.

I was originally trained to follow a specific process in a workshop and seminary class led by the leaders of the CBS movement. In the CBS approach, there is a strong emphasis on participants giving a detailed, accurate retelling of the story immediately after a storyteller tells it. I have removed this as part of my process with adolescents and adults. I discovered that it caused participants to focus on the exact details of the story, with some obsessing about getting every word right. This caused participants to no longer be immersed in the story, but to step outside of it and analyze the details in order to give a chronological account. In place of this, I inserted time to reflect and capture what is meaningful to participants. This keeps them in a state of living in the story through their imaginations, and helps them to pay attention to what God is stirring in their hearts. I also have refined the types of questions I ask, which I will detail in chapter 12. Subsequently, some of the more directive, leading type questions that were a part of the CBS process have been removed. I feel privileged to be a part of the CBS movement. My hope is to continue to help churches and ministries in North America explore Bible storying in their context.

STORYING RENEWS INTEREST IN BIBLE READING

In North America, we're quickly moving away from being a culture centered on literacy and print communications. It's a huge challenge to strive toward being a people who are shaped by the Bible when we live in a culture that's becoming impatient with reading. Therefore, I believe the solution is not to abandon Scripture reading, but rather reintroduce the Bible to our communities of faith through creative means.

That's precisely the role that Bible storying plays in a postliterate culture. Storying is a bridge that helps people see the Bible in a new way—a gateway that fosters imagination and sparks curiosity to explore the rest of the story. I've seen storying effectively renew interest in Bible reading. Many of my students will go back after our storying times and read the Bible accounts on their own, unprompted. They didn't do this to uncover a nugget of truth or the main plot; they read them as true stories—slowing down so they could digest the words and allow the stories to form in their imaginations. The Bible was no longer intimidating, boring or irrelevant to them.

> For the first time I felt like I could relate to the characters in the story. . . I saw the characters as real, plausible and many sided. They became real people doing real things. . . It challenged me to really listen to God and obey his calling.
> —JENNIFER (STUDENT)
>
> I could not stop thinking about the stories. . . it made me want to search for answers.
> —EMILY (STUDENT)

BIBLE STORYING FOSTERS IMPLICATION

When approached as narrative, the Bible Story has a subtle way of getting into our heads and under our skin. At first it seems nonintrusive because it's a faraway story about a distant people. But then it begins to work on us . . . the messages beneath the surface emerge, and we're captivated by its story. We find ourselves inside that story, identifying and empathizing with the characters. It becomes part of our experience and identity—it is now our story.

This is called *implication*, which has a much different meaning from application. Many of us have been trained to think, how does the Bible apply to me? Yet, application literally means, "to put on the surface." Thus, like a Band-Aid or salve, we try to administer the Scriptures to our own situations.

However, to be implicated is to be bound with, wrapped up, and twisted together like the strands of a rope. The word *implicate* comes from the Latin word meaning "folded in." We become intertwined and folded in to the Bible's Story, and it speaks to and informs us about who we are and why we're here.

So our question moves from "How do I apply this to my situation?" to "What does this mean for the way I live my life?" We begin to seek our role in the Bible's story, rather than try to figure out what to do with it.

Implication calls us toward something—to redefine what we know, to a new way of life lived with our community of faith. The Bible's story cultivates hope within us. We begin to envision how we can change our community, our world, and ourselves.

A sophomore girl in my youth group put it this way: "These stories showed me that God gave us a purpose in life—to live for God and not ourselves." A senior guy saw it this way: "It made me realize: I need to live for the Author. God has a story for my life that I'm excited to discover, and I want to share with others. God's amazing Story is what we've been waiting for our entire lives."

> To be implicated is to be bound with, wrapped up, and twisted together like the strands of a rope.

The amazing thing is that application becomes implicit . . . the story informs our experiences and shapes how we should live. We're moved toward restorative action. This happens without us teachers having to provide a list of application points.

One student shared, "I feel that I need to live like I want to be part of God's story." Another noticed, "I saw real life being applied to God's story. . . I thought about how I'm like the characters in God's Story."

The Bible's story is what gives shape and context to our lives as we follow in the ways of Jesus. May we allow it to speak, inform, and reorder our lives so we may discover our role in God's activity in the world.

BIBLE STORYING CULTIVATES SPIRITUAL SKILLS

When I began Bible storying, I expected that along the way my group would gain a better understanding of the Bible. I hoped they would experience God and want to read more from the Bible. But I did not anticipate how this experience would begin to shape my group's theology and identities right in front of me. They were looking for

God—in the Bible and in each other. The language they used was deeper than what I was used to hearing from students—it reached beyond the surface of behavior to the core of their own identities.

> I have seen in myself and in my groups a cultivation of new sensitivities and spiritual awareness, helping us to be more mindful and in tune with God's activity.

As a result of Bible storying, I have seen in myself and in my groups a cultivation of new sensitivities and spiritual awareness, helping us to be more mindful and in tune with God's activity. I see the development of deep listening, reflecting, wondering, observing, creating, noticing, and naming. I have seen participants grow in confidence in their ability to create and articulate. It is as though Bible storying is a kind of group spiritual direction, helping us to explore and ask important and deep questions about the divine and ourselves. We have courage to share and try new expressions of our faith. These are life-long spiritual skills.

MY BASIC BIBLE STORYING PROCESS

REWIND the Story – review previous stories using symbols.

PREPARE for the Story – focus our minds for imaginative listening.

IMAGINE the Story – listen actively to a live telling of a Bible story.

CAPTURE what you notice – record observations by sketching or writing.

CONNECT to your story – share insights through guided dialogue.

* IN THE ECHO THE STORY RESOURCES, A REMIX ACTIVITY IS ADDED BETWEEN CAPTURE AND CONNECT.

In chapter 11 will take an in-depth look at this process.

WHY NOT TELL STORIES STRAIGHT FROM THE BIBLE?

Many of my Echo the Story narratives are very close to modern Bible translations. But most of the Bible—even the narrative parts—is difficult to read aloud, especially conversationally. Here are some of the challenges that prompted me to weave together condensed narratives:

Length—The sheer length of the Bible can be intimidating. Where else do we hand people a book the size of a dictionary and ask them to get excited about studying it? Many Bible stories are dozens of chapters long, making them difficult to unpack in a group setting (especially when people only attend every other week).

Translation—Painstaking efforts have been made to translate and retranslate the Bible, keeping it as close to the source texts as possible. However, anytime a document is translated, there are challenges in making it readable and conversational without sacrificing accuracy. Our English translations aren't very conversational or easy to read—that's why so many paraphrased translations have surfaced.

Language—Even with modern translations, many words and phrases remain unfamiliar to us. Much of what's written in the Bible is tied so closely to past cultures and languages that it's easy for us to get lost and confused. Think about this: it's difficult for us to read and comprehend Shakespeare, which was written in English only a few hundred years ago. The language gap we face with the Bible is even greater.

Tense—Within one story, authors sometimes shift from past to present to future tense. In some cases this is because the accounts were written much later, and the author decided to embed some truths into the text to emphasize different attributes. However, these tense shifts make it difficult to follow some narrative parts of the Bible without getting lost.

Writing Styles—Even if we concentrated on just the Bible's narrative parts, we'd still find that those sections were written in different styles. Some read more like historical accounts, some are poetic, and some are written like a novel. The challenge is that sometimes these styles are mixed together in the same narrative, making them difficult to engage with.

Culture Authorship—Different authors committed the Scripture to written form at different times. So not only is our culture vastly different, but many of the Bible's authors also lived in different cultures and eras. What makes reading the Bible even more challenging is the fact that the authors assumed that those who'd hear or read their words would have an understanding of the cultural traits of that time. Without understanding the background of the author and his intended audience, we can become confused and sidetracked.

IS STORYING BIBLICALLY ACCURATE?

I've met with some ministry leaders who are concerned that storying encourages people to abandon Bible reading. They fear that learning Scripture from condensed Bible stories makes people vulnerable to inaccuracies. I've been told, "People need to learn from the actual Bible, not from paraphrased stories."

I understand this concern—it's true that oral Bible stories can be altered more easily than written or printed stories. I had similar concerns when I began the storying process, especially after seeing my students distort the Bible during our inductive studies. And that's why I put painstaking efforts into the narratives I use. I encourage you to do the same.

I'm relieved to say that my experience has been the opposite of what I initially expected; by developing a culture of careful listening in our group, students are very attentive to the details of the story and protective of the story's essence.

What I've learned is that storying promotes communal correcting. This is when a group helps each other to ensure that important details of the stories are recounted accurately and not overlooked. While dialoguing about one of these stories, I've observed individuals miss key parts or say something that's just flat-out wrong. But each time this happened, the group would respond and correct the person before I could, redirecting the conversation right back to the story. And most of the time, all I needed to say was something like, "What do you think about that?" or "Did the story tell us something about this?"

Communal correcting is easier for the group members to handle and accept. When a leader corrects, group members often want to withdraw from the discussion altogether. But communal correction just becomes a refining part of the conversation. I wonder if a refining process like communal correcting played a role in the preservation of the Scriptures as they were passed down orally from generation to generation?

You may be wondering how oral stories could remain accurate after being retold again and again. This idea seems foreign to us because we've lived in a culture that's been reliant upon printed words. It's easy for us to forget that most people didn't have access to Bibles until a few hundred years ago. That noted, I believe our culture's love affair with words over the past century has influenced many to be hyper-protective of the Bible, appointing themselves gatekeepers to preserve its accuracies and use. Thus, we need to seek God for wisdom, illumination, and guidance to help us see what God desires us to see in the Bible.

HOW I DEVELOP BIBLE STORYING NARRATIVES

Decide *How Many* Stories to Tell

The first question you need to answer is how many stories do you want to develop for Bible storying? That really depends on your context. This may be predetermined for you.

Developing Bible storying sessions is a lot of work, and it can easily get overwhelming. (I know I have been overwhelmed by this task many times.) It may be helpful to start small. The largest scope of sessions I would tackle would be around 36 (a full school year). It may be best to start with one session as a trial and then try a set of four or six. This depends on how ambitious you are and how sold you are on this process!

I always seek to tell a set of stories in a chronology, as this helps support better Bible context and understanding, and it tells one continuous story. Here are some ideas for story sets:

> Six weeks with Moses

> Eight weeks with the Prophets

> Seven weeks in the Life of Jesus

> Twelve week Bible overview (my current favorite, and a resource I released with sparkhouse)

> Thirty-six week Bible overview

You may want put together a chronology of stories that follow a narrative thread like covenant, kingdom, or restoration. I hope this sparks some ideas for you. I have developed Bible overview plans (scope and sequence) ranging from 7 to 120 stories (multi-year). Most of these are still in outline form and not developed into resources yet. If you'd like some ideas or help in deciding which stories to develop, contact me: **michael@wearesparkhouse.org**.

Decide *Which* Stories to Tell

If you are developing a Bible overview, deciding which stories to tell is not easy. You certainly will not be able to tell all of the stories in the Bible (there are several hundred), but you should give careful consideration to covering a full chronology of stories that will give participants a sense of the entire biblical narrative. There is no official formula for this, but do your best to provide a set of stories that will help give a mental timeline or road map of Scripture. Some questions I ask to help narrow my choice of stories are:

> Is (was) the story pivotal to the Jewish people? Is it referenced as a key event elsewhere in the Bible?

> What thread of the biblical story does this story connect with (i.e., covenant, kingdom, redemption, restoration, etc.)?

> How does the story connect with the grand story of Scripture?

Goals and Subjectivity

In developing narratives, my goal is to remain true to the biblical texts, preserving key events and dialogue. I don't try to modernize the stories but tell them chronologically and clearly. I work hard to stitch together the stories so they are accessible, paraphrasing language for readability (I call this "smoothing over the text").

As much as I try to let the Bible texts speak, and as close as my narratives are to modern English translations, they still reflect my own subjectivity. I have a certain lens and perspective through which I, and the community of faith I walk with, look at the scriptures. So, the narratives I stitch together are an invitation to see the Bible in a new way, and in part, to see it in a way that has made sense to me.

I've provided an example of one of my carefully crafted narrative scripts in the Appendices. Additional samples are available at www.wearesparkhouse.org.

> I have to remind myself that I am trying to give participants a palatable a snapshot that will help them see the whole of the Biblical story and ignite curiosity to learn and read more.

Narrative Length

Length and complexity of narrative development depends greatly on the ages you are working with. Generally, I've found it difficult to craft a storying narrative that's less than three hundred words. Dialogue should be the last thing you choose to cut as it best provides the narrative sense and character development of the story. Most of my narratives for elementary age students to adults are in the range of six to eight hundred words, tell-able in five to seven minutes. My longest narrative is around 1,100 words, but that is the epic Exodus story. Most other Bible stories will not hold people's attention for that long. It is hard to be this concise when you are dealing with passages outside of Genesis and the Gospels. Many of the stories are chapters long, and condensing them is painstaking.

Crafting a Storying Narrative

Once I have determined how many and which stories I will be developing, the hard work of stitching together and smoothing over each story begins. This part feels a little strange. . . like I am editing Scripture. I have to remind myself that I am trying to give participants a palatable a snapshot that will help them see the whole of the Biblical story and ignite curiosity to learn and read more. Here are the steps I follow:

1. I read the story for **enjoyment**. I pick a translation that is easy for me to ingest, and I spend time in the story until the characters and setting become visual to me. I try to imagine sounds, tastes, scents, and colors. I don't make any notes; I just slow down and enjoy it.

2. I read the story again with a **noticing eye**. I pay careful attention to the movement of the story, the interaction and dialogue between the characters, and the parts that stand out or seem to be emphasized by the author. I make quick notes of observations and questions that arise.

3. I create a **scripture document**. I cut and paste a modern translation (I like the NLT or the CEV) of the Scripture passage into a word-processing document.

4. I create a **story map**. This is a simple visual diagram identifying the main events, conflict points, climax, resolution, and conclusion of the story. The story map helps me to determine if the portion of scripture I have chosen is too large or too small. Does the shape of my story map look like one story? If I have chosen too large of a chunk of scripture (which is often the case for me), the map will show multiple high peaks and climax points. I need to either divide the passage into multiple stories (sessions) or simplify the story so that it is not too hard to follow.

   This exercise also helps me evaluate what events are essential and nonessential to the overall story. Most often I create story maps in pencil, as I am constantly adjusting lines and reevaluating as I read through the story. It usually takes at least two attempts to settle on a list of the key events I want to make sure are in the story. (See appendix C for a worksheet on how to do this.)

5. I **taper** the Scripture passage. In the scripture document, I begin cutting out (only) whole verses that are not to be a part of the key events that I identified on my story map. This step becomes especially vital when working with stories that are more than a chapter long. What I am left with is groups of verses that, if read together clumsily, tell the story, with some gaps left to fill in.

6. I make a duplicate of the scripture document. I keep a copy that is just the tapered down verses. This is in case I need to reference it later, or if I need to back up and redo a section. Then I use the copy as my working **narrative document**.

7. I **research** pivotal and difficult verses. In my narrative document, I go through the scriptures and look for verses that seem pivotal or challenging. I then compare multiple English Bible translations of these verses to see if there is any variance. Where needed (and especially in spots where English translations vary), I study key words in the original languages. I note my findings in the narrative document, summarizing what seems to be the consensus on the best wording to use for those verses.

8. I look for points that need **historical context**. In my narrative document, I go through the scriptures and highlight verses and sections that may not make sense to my listeners. Then, I do some study on the culture and history of the time and place specific to that passage. For example, people may wonder why it wasn't considered wrong for Abraham to have a child with Sarah's servant. So, I add a brief explanation about how that was a common practice in that day. I will also add in meanings of words or names that add interest. For example, the name Adam means *from the ground*, and also human being.

   Note: For the first time, I now have a team of theological and historical reviewers with doctorates who go through my narratives for sparkhouse. It is frightening and awesome! Once I get through their "vetting" I have so much more confidence that I have honored the text in my narratives.

9. I refine the passage more. This **refinement** includes removing verse numbers and omitting irrelevant names, places, and

redundancies. Scripture is very repetitive in parts. Some of this is for emphasis, but much of it surfaced in translation. A good rule of thumb is to not to introduce more than *five* names of people or places in the story. I also limit proper nouns, geographic locations, genealogies, and technical details. Most of this was immediately relevant to the story's original hearers, but it would take a lot of time for you to build context and significance for your group. At this stage, I try to cut the story down to 1,000 words or less if possible.

> A good rule of thumb is to not to introduce more than five names of people or places in the story.

Note: Be careful not to cut too much dialogue. Dialogue and character descriptions are sparse in many of the biblical accounts. Removing too much of these elements will strip the stories of their narrative dynamic, making them feel more like a list than a story.

10. I **stitch** together the remaining portions. After editing the story, there will be gaps in between the story's parts. To make it read more coherently, I write bridges that connect the segments and fill in the gaps. I work to make these extremely succinct and nondescript, so that they blend in. I use the term *stitching* for this act because it describes my desire for the process. I am pulling together portions and creating seams that are hopefully undetectable. I want to allow the text of the Bible to speak for itself, as though the ancients were telling it. I believe the stories are already there, but centuries of translation and reinterpretation have created some layers of language that make these stories hard to read aloud.

11. I **smooth** over the rough edges. Next I go back through my narrative and read it for clarity. How does it sound read aloud? What parts feel unnatural or awkward? I smooth over these parts, simplifying language and making the story easily readable. I am careful to make the language seems fluid and idiomatic, avoiding overly contemporary language. I do not add a lot of detail or verbiage. The best storytelling is succinct.

12. I get **feedback**. I have other people read it over a few times and send me feedback. Based on their feedback, I may have to back

up a few steps and fix part of the story. I may need to cut or add portions. After these edits, I go back through the story and work on developing dialogue questions (details on how to do this are in the next section).

> Appendix C is a worksheet that walks you through a more basic approach to this process.

HOW I DEVELOP STORYING QUESTIONS

Sequencing Questions

I always begin with wondering questions because they naturally flow out of an imaginative experience of the story. They are disarming and allow participants freedom to safely express feelings and wonderings with the group. Remembering and interpreting questions follow, ordered by the events in the story. I conclude with a connecting question that turns the focus toward "How is this story our story?"

> I believe the stories are already there, but centuries of translation and reinterpretation have created some layers of language that make these stories hard to read aloud.

Storying questions are designed to be like scaffolding that help build lifelong spiritual skills of wondering, reflecting, noticing, naming, and synthesizing. Storying questions help instill in us an inclination to look for God in the scriptures and in each other.

I will go more in-depth in chapter 12 about each type of question and its use in Bible storying.

Basic Storying Questions I Use

What stood out to you from the story? What did the story make you wonder about? What did you notice about the characters in the story and their relationships? How would you describe the characters in the story?

What did you notice about God (Jesus) from this story? How is this story our story? Appendix D is a worksheet that helps you develop Bible storying questions.

ADAPTING OTHER BIBLE NARRATIVES

For those who simply don't have the time to develop their own Bible narratives, I have a list of some sources you could use in the Appendices. Most will take some adaptation. A few good resources are Zondervan's *The Story: Read the Bible as One Seamless Story from Beginning to End*; Nick Page's *The Big Story: What Actually Happens in the Bible*; Zondervan's *The Jesus Storybook Bible* by Sally Lloyd Jones; and *Echo the Story*, a line of Bible storying resources I am developing for **www.wearesparkhouse.org**. If you choose to buy my Bible storying resources, thank you. But I hope you sincerely know that this book is not intended as a bait and switch to get you to buy a product.

In my Bible storying resources you may find word choices or parts that do not resonate with you or your understanding of the Bible. My hope is that you would prayerfully make changes that you and your congregation agree with, and that connect your community to experience the biblical narrative in the deepest ways. I'll be the first to tell you that I don't have the Bible all figured out. My narratives probably don't contain every detail that every reader would want in them. They are a work in progress, and I do appreciate your patience and support.

I have provided a **Creating an Environment for Storying Worksheet** in the appendices to help you brainstorm environment and creative reflection options. Be sure to read the section about Learning Styles in chapter 9 and the section on Capture What You Notice in chapter 11 to provide context for this worksheet.

SETTINGS FOR BIBLE STORYING

Storying is effective in a variety of settings: weekly gatherings, retreats, small groups, camps, and so on. I've had the opportunity to lead Bible storying in all of these settings, and they all have advantages and challenges. The best settings are those in which ample time is allowed for the storying process.

The most challenging (and least effective) use of storying has been when I tried to cover a lot of stories in a short amount of time. I've had a few opportunities when I was asked to cover the entire biblical storyline in two days or less. To do that well, you have to cover seven or eight narratives at a minimum. As interactive as storying is, telling that many stories in that short a time feels like information overload.

Weekly studies and weeklong events are better settings for storying than retreats. I've helped create a weeklong interactive event called Merge that takes students through twelve key Bible narratives. (For more information go to **www.mergeevent.com**.) Should you need some guidance while planning how to use storying in your setting, I would love to help. You can email me at **michael@wearesparkhouse.org**.

STORYING WITH LARGER GROUPS

Storying is designed to allow everyone time to share observations about the story. This creates some challenges when working with larger groups. Over the last several years I've been experimenting with different ways to create environments for storying with larger groups. If you plan to implement this approach in a large group, I would love to brainstorm some creative solutions with you.

As a general guideline, if I have more than twenty-five participants, I'll divide them into smaller groups. This is essential to allow time and opportunity for everyone to share. The following are some approaches to structuring storying for large groups that I've found effective:

Large Group Storytelling, Small Group Dialogue

Many of the larger groups I've worked with lead storytelling with the entire group together, then break into small groups for the dialogue. They train facilitators to lead small group dialogues. This approach to storying works well—in fact, it's the same approach we've taken with our Merge student event. The challenge is finding and training good volunteer dialogue leaders. (Should you need help, this is my specialty—I spend a lot of time working with churches to help train volunteers to lead storying groups.)

Participant-led "Buzz" Groups

The term buzz groups has been used in educational training for decades, and comes from the idea that students within a classroom turn to each other and form smaller groups. The "buzz" is the sound of the discussion from around the room as groups interact with each other.

When storying with a large group and you are the only teacher familiar with the process, buzz groups are the best solution I have found for dialogue. The storytelling is lead by the teacher from the front with the entire group together. Then, retelling and dialogue is done in buzz groups of four to six people. If necessary for supervision, all of the buzz groups can remain in the same room.

Buzz groups do not require a facilitator, as all instructions and questions are provided by the teacher from the front of the room. This is often best done by using a slide presentation and video projector or television. Or, you could provide handouts for each group. Each buzz group selects a spokesperson to share some of their groups' responses. A time limit is set for the dialogue—and possibly for each question—depending on how much structure the teacher feels is needed.

Thought must be given as to who will be in each buzz group. Teachers may want to assign groups to help keep the discussion focused. The teacher should "float" from group to group to motivate better involvement, clarify questions, and spread enthusiasm around the room. After the assigned time is up for the buzz groups, the teacher should facilitate a time for a spokesperson to share responses from each group.

CREATING AN ENVIRONMENT FOR STORYING

In almost any culture, the most personal place of communication is at our dining tables, especially around a meal. Meeting there speaks of relationship, equality, and family. That is the kind of environment we should aspire to for Bible storying: To create a safe place for us to share openly, be encouraged, and feel loved.

That doesn't necessarily mean you have to sit around a table—but it would be great if you could! You should try to sit in a circle where everyone can make eye contact and hear each other well. Do everything you can to create a place where each person feels like an equal.

We moved our group from meeting in the youth room at the church to meeting in a home—away from all of the games and hip atmosphere. I wanted our students to see that youth group was not a program to attend, but rather a community—a family—that we can be a part of. About eighteen of us would sit in a circle in the living room of one of our students' houses. We'd light a candle to symbolize entering into a sacred time—the beginning of the storytelling.

I used to sit on a stool and use a music stand for my notes when I told the stories. After thinking about this for a while, I realized that those items differentiate me from the rest of the group—literally setting me above them. So I got rid of them. It wasn't that big of a deal for me to sit in a chair and hold my notes. I want the group to know that I'm a co-learner and a full participant in learning from the Bible.

> In almost any culture, the most personal place of communication is at our dining tables, especially around a meal. Meeting there speaks of relationship, equality, and family.

We're already fighting the notion that only experts have something meaningful to say about the Bible. Students are used to hearing the "right answers." We must do all we can to remove any obstacles that may hinder our students from sharing.

I understand that many of our meeting spaces present some unique challenges. For instance, some of us have large groups, and we have to get creative to figure out how to create safe places for open dialogue.

The environment you create communicates a lot. If we meet in a room where one person stands on stage with a spotlight and a microphone and the rest of the group sits facing that person, then what might that communicate? To me, it communicates that I'm not expected to participate, but spectate. This is the opposite of the environment we should strive to create.

ACTVIVITY IDEAS TO USE BEFORE STORYING

Before you begin storying with your group, plan an activity to help them think about their favorite stories and what makes them so engaging. It could be as simple as discussing your own favorite stories or viewing a clip from a movie with a powerful story and discussing it.

My friend Seth showed a short segment from the middle of one of the Lord of the Rings movies. Then he asked his students to describe the events that led up to that scene. Seth made the point that we need to know the entire story—from the beginning—in order to really understand each scene.

One of the activities I start almost every year with is a Life Storyboard. I have participants use a pen or pencil to divide a piece of paper into 6 equal squares. Then I have them draw a picture in each box to describe the following:

1. My childhood and life growing up...

2. The most important people in my life and why

3. The most difficult challenge I've faced...

4. How I would describe my faith...

5. The best ways to describe me are . . .

6. What I hope to see in my future . . .

They write a word, phrase, or sentence under each snapshot to help explain what you they've drawn. I encourage my group not to worry about artistic ability or about making the pictures too detailed. After they complete this (it takes about twenty minutes) I have them share their story with the group.

QUESTIONS FOR REFLECTION AND DISCUSSION

› *How might you use Bible storying in your ministry?*

› *What do you think is most challenging about developing Bible storying sessions?*

› *What outcome would you hope for if you were to use Bible storying with your group?*

› *What do you think is essential for creating the right environment for Bible storying?*

A TRUE STORY ABOUT STORYING

My deep love for story and for God's timeless truths drew me to the storying process. I'd done all kinds of research on communicating in stories, in wondering, and in questions, but I had yet to experience it. I knew storying would be a great thing, but I didn't realize how deep it would go. Storying connected with my soul—deep into that place where most other things don't have the power to touch.

My first experience with storying was during a training session with Michael in which we were learning how to lead this process. I felt as though this was the first time I'd been able to experience God's Story—able to wonder, to think, to process in a new way. I fell totally in love with God as the creator and the greatest Artist. I saw more and understood more about God. I experienced the emotion that God expressed in the stories—anger, lament, joy, despair, amazement, hope. The story became a whole experience—not divided in pieces and packaged. It was complete.

We recently began storying with the students at our church, and they've been blown away! Most of the students I work with have never really been to church. But right before my eyes, I've seen seeds being planted and real growth taking place. We've had discussions about the Bible that are incredibly deep—deeper than I had in Bible college. They were taken on a journey into the Story of God, and they were captivated by its complexity and beauty.

I feel as though storying helps free the power of the Bible to speak. I've seen hardened, rebellious kids' eyes light up as they frantically search for paper and pen so they can start writing down what the group is discussing. I'm watching teenagers fall in love with Jesus. They're connecting like I've never seen before. They're realizing they have a place in this amazing story. God's Story is helping our students grow in a deep understanding of God and an unshakable relationship with him.

—**HEATHER FOWLER**, VOLUNTEER IN CHICAGO, ILLINOIS

CHAPTER ELEVEN

THE BIBLE STORYING PROCESS

The following is a Bible storying process that I've used many times. Ideally, it should be used in a time slot when you have at sixty to ninety minutes to meet. What's important is that you allow enough time so you're not hurrying through the process. The duration below is adapted for a youth or adult group.

Part	Suggested Duration
REWIND the Story	10 minutes
PREPARE for the Story	5 minutes
IMAGINE the Story	5 minutes
CAPTURE what you notice	15 minutes
CONNECT to your story	15 minutes

* IN THE ECHO THE STORY RESOURCES A REMIX ACTIVITY IS ADDED BETWEEN CAPTURE AND CONNECT.

REPETITION IN EACH SESSION

When I lead storying, I follow the same process every session. For some, following the same pattern session after session appears to be boring. In our culture we have so many choices in content and entertainment, we struggle to follow any kind of rhythm or ritual. What participants may not realize is that this repetition and rhythm fosters safety and creates boundaries that will actually help to free up imaginations to go deeper into the stories. Many will need encouragement to invest in the process in order to begin to see the benefits.

Eventually, participants will get into the rhythm, and begin to truly listen and think deeply about the story. Along the way, they will cultivate new kinds of spiritual skills and sensitivities, as the process guides them to assign meaning to their experiences of the Bible, and to look for God in Scripture and in one another.

ADJUSTING STORYING FOR YOUNGER GROUPS

For children and pre-teens (and some junior high groups) you will need to adapt this process to better meet their development capacities. Please give careful consideration to adjusting the following areas:

Language: make sure that the language in your Story narrative is accessible for the ages you are working with. Find examples of resources that have navigated this well to assist you, like Zondervan's The Jesus Storybook Bible and sparkhouse's Holy Moly and Spark Bible. Some of the language of the questions may also need to be adjusted. For example, "What did you notice about God?" could be changed to "What is God like in this story?"

Capture Stations: children are accustomed to choice and variety in their learning paths. Consider adding Capture stations that use various mediums, including: acting, clay, listening stations, paints, group projects, reenactment with figures, and so on. Consider extending the Capture time to at least twenty or thirty minutes of your session.

Connect dialogue: While it is important that you still provide time for your group to verbally express their wonderings and observations, this part could be cut down to ten minutes or less. Children do not have the life experience to relate to or abstract abilities to decipher meaning and application in the same way youth and adults do, so dialogue may need to be limited to a few key questions.

> Bible storying takes a different approach, helping participants surface and explore their own unique observations, and find meaning together with their group.

ADJUSTING TO A NEW WAY OF LEARNING

Traditional Western approaches to education have conditioned people to respond to questions with answers they think the teacher is looking for. This approach has also guided how many churches teach. Bible storying takes a different approach, helping participants surface and explore their own unique observations, and find meaning together with their group.

It may take some time for your group to reorient to this learner-centered approach. The idea that their observations are what will teach the group may be new to them.

Keep encouraging your group and letting them know how valuable their insights are. Everyone's reflections and creative expressions matter and help the entire group have a richer experience of God.

BIBLE STORYING SESSION DETAILS

I've provided an example session, the story of Creation, in the appendices. Additional samples are available at **www.wearesparkhouse.org**.

1. REWIND the Story

Reviewing previous stories should be fast-paced and fun. I call this part REWIND because it suggests that we will be rewinding the story in out minds and (quickly) playing it back. Think of this like an episode recap from a television show that gets you up to speed on what happened in the story, even if you missed a week.

> Symbols are powerful mnemonic devices that provide a visual marker that help our minds call on memories and experiences of the story.

Rewinding the story is especially important if you're meeting weekly. In addition to triggering our memories about previous stories, Rewind also helps us make connections between the stories and see how each story fits into a larger narrative.

During Rewind, we focus on the symbols from the stories we've already told. I will typically ask participants to identify the story that goes with each of them. I might say (pointing to each symbol) something like: "Can anyone tell me—in twenty seconds or less—what happened in *this* story?" I try to get lots of people involved in this activity and enjoy it.

Symbols are powerful mnemonic devices that provide a visual marker that help our minds call on memories and experiences of the story. I had one of our students draw the symbol for the week and then we hung them up in order on our youth room wall. My symbols are intentionally simple so anyone can draw and remember them (see below). You may even want to see if your group can come up with their own symbols. Have fun with this and be creative.

SOME OF THE ORIGINAL SYMBOLS I USED:

SOME OF THE CURRENT SYMBOLS I USE:

If you do Bible storying for more than a few month stretch, I'd encourage you to plan one or two sessions that solely focus on review. These are important moments for your group to be able to look back, remember, and think about what they're learning from the stories as a whole.

Using media for Rewind: Though not required, I have begun to use video segments to help us rewind the story. Included with Echo the Story, these resources are fast-paced, animated video segments called The Story So Far that bring to life the story symbols to tell the biblical story.

2. PREPARE for the Story
For the PREPARE part of the session, I ask participants to quickly draw their own version of the story symbol for the new story we are about to tell. This activity helps embed the symbol in participants' minds, and turns their thoughts toward the story I will be telling in that session. I give participants blank sketchbooks, or with my Echo the Story resources, a customized sketch journal is provided.

After we draw the current story symbol, we slow down and prepare to listen to the story with our imaginations. Participants come to each gathering with varying levels of personal distraction—tiredness, stress, hyperactivity, and so on. The storying process is very repetitive, and some people who are accustomed to constant stimulation from media tend to lose focus easily. You'll need to intentionally help them refocus and coach them to be attentive listeners every session.

You need to ready your group for the storytelling time, letting them know this is sacred time for listening and entering into the story—a slower, more focused time. Set the tone for this, letting students know that it's a special time and they'll need to work hard at concentrating and getting into "storying mode." To help them get started, you may want to light a candle to signify storying as a holy practice.

Make sure you tell participants that there will be no talking during the storytelling. They should plan to find a focal point in the room to look at, close their eyes, or take notes—whatever will help them focus completely on the story. Encourage your group to further engage through imaginative listening. Imaginative listening is simply using your imagination to picture the story in your mind—like you would a movie—and imagine that you're in the scene.

Let your group know that they'll get a chance to capture what they noticed from the story and share it with the group. Knowing that sharing is expected often helps improve the students' attentiveness because they want to be ready if called upon.

Right before you begin telling the story, ask participants to take a quiet moment to slow down, clear their minds, close their eyes, take a deep breath, and whisper a prayer asking God to show them something new in the story.

Repetition is good. Plan to refocus your group every time you meet. It may seem redundant to you, but trust me—the more you help them focus and encourage them to pay attention, the greater their participation and engagement. Groups that skip the Prepare part often lose focus and come to the story too casually, causing the entire process to go off track.

Using reflective metaphors to prepare: Though not required, I often use a short metaphor or analogy to help my group think about the Bible in an imaginative way. I've provided an example of this in the sample lesson in appendix G.

3. IMAGINE the Story

The IMAGINE part of Bible storying is a live reading (telling) of a narrative. Storytellers should not just drably read words off a page, but work to bring those words to life with their voice. This requires putting energy and emotion into the reading without drawing attention to yourself.

Bible storying tales may be (somewhat) verbally dramatic, but should not be visually dramatic. The hope is that participants will be creating the story in their minds, not watching you and your movements. For this reason, I have begun to move to the side or the back of the room when I tell a story. I encourage participants to close their eyes, find a focal point in the room, sketch or write ideas related to the story.

Here are some important reminders for storytellers:

Know the story. The more you read the story aloud in your preparation, the more you will connect with it. Spend time in the story until the characters and setting become visual to you. Use the Story Map activity in the Appendices to help better connect with the story.

Don't skip the PREPARE part of the session. It is critical to helping participants get in the right frame of mind for the story. If you skip it, it may be much harder for your group to focus.

Tell the story from beginning to end—don't stop! You'll cause confusion by stopping to answer a question, teach, clarify, give application, or make an observation in the middle the story.

Stick to the script. Craft story scripts ahead of time (or use someone else's), and stick to them. Don't embellish or riff. Remember, I encourage two readings of each story (back to back). Participants benefit from consistency. If you change or skip parts they will focus on those parts instead of entering in to the story.

Be genuinely animated and enthusiastic! You need to bring energy to this process. But don't overdo it!

Be aware of your pacing. Pacing involves both the volume and rate at which you speak and the progression of the action in the story. Dialogue slows a story's pace, while narrating action speeds it up. I change pacing and slightly alter my tone when reading my dialogue.

Avoid joking and sarcasm. They can project a very different meaning from the biblical meaning you believe you're projecting.

Be patient with the process. At first, some in your group may feel that this approach is too basic. After you're a few stories into it, they'll realize how much there is to be learned and get into the rhythm of this different way of experiencing the Bible.

Relax and be yourself. Develop your own style—one that you're comfortable with.

Team up. Ask different people from your ministry that are good at telling stories to narrate.

You can do it! With a little work and patience, most anyone can be read a Bible story with inflection and emotion that engages listeners.

Using visuals during the *imagine* part: Though not required, I often will project an image for a focal point while telling the story. I try to find images that help to create a visual backdrop for the story, like scenery for a play. I never use images of people or modern day locations, as their descriptiveness is too distracting. Backdrops should be nondescript and abstract to encourage participants to focus on creating the story in their minds. I mostly use images of water, skies, trees, fire and landscapes.

4. CAPTURE What You Notice

Immediately after the story I ask participants to take a quiet moment to replay the story in their mind. This twenty-second pause creates a bridge between the storytelling and the CAPTURE activity, helping participants stay connected to their imaginations.

Following this moment, I let participants know that we will be hearing the story again, this time from a reader of the opposite gender from the first storyteller. Different voices help people to listen with fresh ears.

There are many books and resources on how to become a good storyteller. Here are two I've found helpful:

> *The Art of Storytelling: Easy Steps to Presenting an Unforgettable Story.* John Walsh, Moody, 2003

> *The Storyteller's Start-Up Book: Finding, Learning, Performing, and Using Folk-Tales.* Margaret Read MacDonald, August House, 1993

While participants are listening to the second telling of the story, I encourage them to capture what they are seeing in the story (what stands out to them). I encourage them to choose from some options:

Sketch scenes that stood out to you. Draw the story as you see it. This could be a picture of a scene, or several on a page, like a storyboard.

Write about what stood out to you. Put yourself in this story. Write about what you see. Journal, write a poem, a song, a spoken word piece, or a short story.

Listen for what stands out to you. Listen carefully with your imagination (don't fall asleep!). Put yourself in this story. Think about what stands out to you and how you will share it during our upcoming dialogue time.

I let participants know that this capturing time is quiet, but they may move about the room, sit or kneel or lie down. This gives people an opportunity to get in a different posture that may help them to better listen, reflect or draw. People know their bodies better than we do, and they appreciate the opportunity to stretch or give themselves more space.

After the second telling is complete, I let participants know they have two minutes to finish capturing what they noticed in the story before we begin sharing.

If I see participants who are not taking this seriously, who lack focus, or who are struggling to engage, I use affirmation to challenge them. I remind them that their gifts and input matter—that they help teach the group and me. I try to be specific in affirming aspects that I like that participants create or write.

Why offer participants choice? Simply put, choice unlocks learning in a way nothing else can. A study in the *Journal of Education Psychology* highlights the importance of choice in learning:

> I let participants know that we will be hearing the story again, this time from a reader of the opposite gender from the first storyteller. Different voices help people to listen with fresh ears.

Providing students with choices increases student interest, engagement, and learning; that students spend more time and effort on the learning task if they are offered choices; and that giving students choices helps build other important skills, such as self-regulation. In particular, teachers suggested that choice was especially beneficial for students with low interest and little motivation for a particular task.[1]

> At the core of spiritual formation is a wrestling with, owning and naming that in which God is stirring inside of us.

Why emphasize sketching and art? At the core of spiritual formation is a wrestling with, owning and naming that in which God is stirring inside of us. Articulation becomes important because it provides us an opportunity to express that struggle and stirring, and to begin to understand and own it more fully. We all articulate best in different ways. For many, words don't express the depths of our observations and inklings as well as images do. My hope in providing opportunities for sketching and creating in the Bible storying process is that it will open up a portal for some to express their experience of God and the Bible in meaningful ways. Philosopher Henryk Skolimowski affirms the power of creative articulation:

"The power of creation is the power of articulation. When painters such as the Impressionist began to see reality in a new way, they invariably articulate it in a fresh way. Without a novel articulation there is no new seeing. Every new creative act is a new act of articulation. Creation is the process; articulation is the product."[2]

Why encourage journaling? Like sketching, journaling connects with many who find it important to use words to express their experiences. In the book *Helping Students Learn in a Learner-Centered Environment,* educator Terry Doyle expresses the power that reflective journaling has:

"Reflective journaling greatly enhances students' understanding and recall because the very fact of writing causes them to move their ideas from the abstract world inside the brains into the concrete world outside their brains. Writing causes them to translate this new learning into their own words and produce it in a clear and

Creating the Environment for Storying

I have provided a worksheet in the appendices to help you brainstorm environment and more creative reflection options. Be sure to read the section about learning styles in chapter 9 to provide context for this worksheet.

organized manner, which will only be possible if they understand what they've learned."[3]

5. REMIX

In some of the Echo the Story resources I have added a remix activity that follows the capture segment. This is not required to lead a Bible storying session, but may enhance the experience for certain kinds of learners.

These activities are provided in a participant Sketch Journal. These activities extend the opportunity to capture observations from the story through more structured activities that encourage participants to retell part of the story in their own way. In order to connect with different learning styles, each Remix section gives participants a choice between either a drawing or creative writing activity. These activities have been specially designed to spark creativity, interact with Scripture text, connect with multiple learning styles, provide choice and ownership, and prompt participants to reenter the story. To see a sample of one REMIX activity, download the Echo the Story Sketch Journal sample at **www.wearesparkhouse.org**.

6. CONNECT to Your Story

During the CONNECT segment, I guide my group in a dialogue using intentionally crafted questions that help prompt participants to share their own observations from the story. Dialogue is where deeper meaning emerges and the story starts to become our story. The goal is not to direct people to a point of application or for everyone to give the same answer—it is to spark wonder and careful observation of the story. In the midst of curiosity, connections and applications surface naturally.

Storying dialogue focuses on:

> **Wondering Questions** to spark imaginative responses:
> "When you listened to this story, what did you see or sense?"

> **Interpreting Questions** to synthesize observations:
> "What did you notice about God in this story?"

> **Remembering Questions** to recall details:
> "What did Adam say when he first saw Eve?"

> **Connecting Questions** to stir personal implications:
> "How is this story our story? How is it your story?"

The goal of the dialogue time is listening, discovery, and connection. Our role is to help participants engage fully in the process of learning. Through inspired dialogue we help students activate their imaginations and explore what God has for them in his story. That means we value what the story means for each individual, rather than focusing on what we feel is relevant. This is hard for us to do. We want others to come to the same understanding we have. The goal of storying is never to come to a consensus on what the story means. It's to come to the Bible as humble learners, with awe and wonder, embracing the mystery and complexity, expecting to encounter the Divine.

> Through inspired dialogue we help students activate their imaginations and explore what God has for them in his story.

Sarah Arthur, in her book *The God-Hungry Imagination*, challenges us to "respect what the Holy Spirit is doing in the imaginations of your students. Don't try to manipulate, interpret, or explain the story away. You cannot forcibly open ears. Moreover, you may not be around when they begin to understand what the story is about. . . . Allow a story to have multiple layers of meaning, more like an onion than a puzzle. And give your students the freedom and luxury to unpeel the onion at their own pace."[4]

Good news! The next chapter focuses entirely on how to best lead a Bible storying dialogue.

QUESTIONS FOR REFLECTION AND DISCUSSION

> *What do you think it takes to lead Bible storying well?*

> *What do you think is the most challenging part of leading Bible storying?*

> *How is Bible storying different than most approaches to the Bible?*

> *What new approaches will you try as a result of this chapter?*

A TRUE STORY ABOUT STORYING

It's no secret today that many people do not read the Bible, youth included. They may know some of the stories in there, but only vaguely. And they often don't know how any of them are connected to each other or what any of them mean for us today, if anything.

I once had a young girl in our confirmation program ask her leader, "So Jesus and Moses are brothers?" This was a girl who had been in our confirmation program already for a year.

After hearing this, I became convinced of the importance of teaching our young people the Bible story. I wanted them to know the stories, how they were connected, who the characters were, what the characters were up to and why . . . I wanted the Bible to come alive to them. I wanted them to see how God had been interacting with this world since the creation and what that means for us, today. I wanted them to discover what in the world this bible had to say to them and their friends.

I wanted students to learn the story in community, find themselves in it, and then begin to live it!

When I discovered storying, I discovered an innovative, creative, and fresh approach that creates spaces for people to encounter the story of God, learn how it implicates them, and uncover how it might just change their everyday life. Students began to explore the story and do theology. It was empowering and revelatory for many of them.

I will always approach the bible, learning, and theology differently thanks to my experiences with storying.

—**RYAN BRALEY**, YOUTH MINISTER FROM ELK RIVER, WISCONSIN

CHAPTER TWELVE

LEADING AN EFFECTIVE DIALOGUE

Dialogue time is the solidifying piece in the storying process. Dialogue is where connections are made, key truths emerge, and the story becomes "our" story. Dialogue is the key to effective Bible storying.

> Dialogue is where connections are made, key truths emerge, and the story becomes "our" story.

Questions are used to direct the participants to discover personal insights from the stories. In order to keep the group focused, a dialogue time always points to the story that was just told and its connection to the previous stories in the chronology.

The Bible storying dialogue is the main focus of the Connect segment. I have committed an entire chapter to this because of how important it is to the process.

Note: the person leading the dialogue can be different than the storyteller. Larger groups may have one storyteller but then break into smaller groups with many dialogue leaders.

STORYING DIALOGUE IS INTENTIONAL AND OPEN-ENDED

Storying dialogue is open-ended in the sense that many questions have more than one correct response. Open-ended doesn't mean that the process is without guidance and direction. In fact, storying dialogue is extremely intentional. The dialogue questions in my narratives are carefully crafted and placed in a specific order to help participants think deeply about the events and characters in each story—especially about the nature of God.

Because of storying's open-ended approach, some may fear it can become relativistic. On the contrary, storying dialogue isn't a loose discussion where any response is valid. The Bible stories provide the boundaries for interpretative missteps to be challenged. Participants are gently asked, "What did the story say about that?" and the group helps keep discussions on track through communal correcting (see the section in chapter 10, Is Storying Biblically Accurate? for more on communal correcting).

SETTING EXPECTATIONS WITH YOUR GROUP

Dialogue time should have a different feel from the reflective tone of the Imagine and Capture segments. This is a time in which participation is critical, and the energy must be high. You want to provide a healthy level of anticipation in your group, letting them know that you have high expectations and you value their input.

1. **Share Your Hopes**

   Before you begin your first dialogue time, share your hopes for the group. Let them know that you believe God will teach you and the rest of the group through them. Express your desire to be a co-learner in the process. Emphasize that everyone is expected to participate, and that each person's observations matter—this is not about "right" answers; it's about sharing observations and coming to shared meaning together (see the section on The Seventy Faces of Torah in Chapter 8. Let them know that this process will require some effort to focus and use our imaginations.

2. **Set Some Boundaries**

   Any good group dialogue must have boundaries to ensure that everyone has a voice. Before (or instead of) giving your list of boundaries, you may want to have your group work together to come up with their own list, asking them: "What do you think it would take for us to have a great dialogue time together?"

   Here are some of the basics:

   › No jumping ahead to future stories—only connecting to stories we've already covered in the chronology.

   › Everyone's expected to share in the dialogue—without being subjected to interruptions or put-downs.

> Most of the questions center on things you notice, connections you make, and questions you have.

> It's also okay for you (and me) to say, "I don't know."

> You may ask each other questions about the story—in fact, I encourage this!

You'll need to regularly revisit the list of boundaries with your group—especially during the first few weeks. Remember, repetition is good!

TYPES OF DIALOGUE QUESTIONS

The questions I use for Bible storying are designated as wondering, interpreting, remembering, and connecting. The wondering and interpreting questions are divergent, meaning that responses can go in a myriad of directions with many acceptable answers. About 90 percent of the questions I ask are divergent wondering and interpreting questions. Remembering and connecting questions are convergent, meaning that they draw participants toward particular responses and specific answers.

1. **Wondering Questions (Sensing)**
   These questions help participants share what they're noticing about the story and connect with their sensory experience of the story. Wondering questions bring energy to your group, inviting and inspiring new and creative insights. These questions are intentionally expansive, opening up imagination to the possibilities of the story. They inspire wonder, curiosity and awe.

   Here are some sample wondering questions:

   > "What stood out to you from the story?

   > "How would you feel if you were in the boat with Jesus?"

   > "What does this story make you wonder about?"

Important: I always begin with at least one wondering question! It's essential that you do this. Why? you may ask. Because wondering questions:

> Set a tone that you're not looking for "Sunday school" answers

> Give a sense of freedom that the participants' observations and feelings matter

> Help the listeners think about the stories in the realm of reality

> Allow participants to use their imagination and creativity—areas unreached in most small groups

> Make it okay to wonder and have questions about the Bible

> Give participants a sense of freedom to explore the stories instead of trying to dissect them.

About 90 percent of the questions I ask are divergent wondering and interpreting questions.

Wondering questions have helped disarm my participants and allowed them to use their imaginations. When participants asked questions about the story out of wonder (for instance, "Who was Cain afraid would attack him if he and his family were the first humans?"), I wouldn't give my opinion or an expert's answer. I'd just affirm them, saying, "That's a great question; I wonder about that, too." This took some getting used to for the participants because they expected me, the Bible teacher, to give them all the answers. By allowing this kind of wondering and tension, we provided space for imagination and curiosity to explore the stories and relate to them out of our own experiences.

2. Remembering Questions (Facts)

These questions help participants recount specific details from the story. These questions promote comprehension by encouraging participants to put what they remember into words. When asking remembering questions, you're looking for participants to recount what happened in the story.

Some sample remembering questions...

> "What did God create in this story?"

> "What were the consequences of Adam and Eve's decision?"

> What did Jesus say to the man lying on the mat?"

Important: I use these questions sparingly. On occasion we will get stuck on a detail in the story, and I will use these questions to try and get us back on track. These questions help to encourage "communal correcting." This is when a group helps each other to ensure that important details of the stories are recounted accurately and not overlooked. (See the section in chapter 10, "Is Storying Biblically Accurate?" for more on communal correcting).

3. Interpreting Questions (Meaning)

These questions help participants ascribe meaning to their observations. They foster abstract conceptualization—the ability to relate to and theorize about the experience of the story. When asking interpretive questions, you're looking for participants to attribute value and give names to their experiences from the story. Here are some sample interpreting questions:

> › "How would you describe Abraham from this story?"

> › "What was God's relationship with Moses like?"

> › What did you notice about God from the story?"

Important: We need to teach others to interpret the Bible—not just acquire Bible knowledge. Interpretive questions help build interpretive skills. They help us build a theology and learn how to learn from the Bible. Theologian Andy Root emphasizes the need to cultivate interpretive skills in teens:

> **We need to teach others to interpret the Bible—not just acquire Bible knowledge. Interpretive questions help build interpretive skills.**

[Adolescents] are expected to acquire biblical knowledge, but are rarely invited to be interpreters of the text—even though their very ontological state, their very way of being in the world, demands that they constantly interpret. It is no wonder that the Bible never sticks, because we never allow the Bible to touch anything deep enough in their being to hold. The goal is not that adolescents "know the Bible" but that they encounter the God who makes Godself known through the Bible. The goal is for young people to be equipped to interpret the Bible . . . and use the Bible to interpret the action of God in their lives and in the world.[1]

4. Connecting Questions (Implications)

These questions stir participants to think about how the story connects to their own lives. I provide several of these questions for each story, but I generally choose one to center on for our connection time. When asking connecting questions, allow ample time for your group to process and respond. I often give my group time to write down their responses and share them in smaller groups.

When responding to connecting questions, some participants tend to be too general and some get "preachy," telling the rest of the group how they need to apply the story. Challenge participants to instead share *personal* applications and meaning. It also helps if you ask participants to try and use "I" and "me" instead of "you" or "we" when sharing.

Here are some sample connecting questions:

> "How is this story *our* story? How is this story *your* story?"

> "What do you believe it means to be created in the image of God?"

> "How did this story challenge or encourage you?"

KEYS TO STORYING DIALOGUE

There's an art to leading a dialogue well—it's a careful balance of pacing, listening, connecting observations, and asking good follow-up questions. Storying dialogue is a process that's difficult to describe, and it takes practice to do it effectively. Here are some things that are important to keep in mind as you begin this journey:

Allow Time for Thinking and Sharing

Don't be afraid of silence. People need time to think about the question before expressing their thoughts out loud. By waiting after you ask a question, you cultivate an expectation that you really want participants to thoughtfully respond.

I have to work hard at this. I get impatient when my group isn't answering right away, and I almost immediately begin to rephrase the question or call on someone. I need to slow down a bit and put myself in the place of the participants. If you relate to my impatience, try this approach next time you lead a discussion:

> Begin by stating your question in a relaxed and confident manner. When you finish, start counting silently to yourself, "One thousand and one, one thousand and two," and so on until you get to "ten." This isn't a long period of silence, though it will seem like an eternity. Scan the room slowly, remaining calm and relaxed, as you count. Most often you won't have to wait this long for the first response. If your group isn't used to open-ended discussions, expect to count all the way to ten several times during the first few weeks of meeting.

> If no one has responded when you finish your count to ten, remain calm and rephrase the question in a shorter, clearer form. Send the nonverbal message, "I'm comfortable with waiting; I can wait here all day!" This will help prompt participants to respond. Then begin your second count to ten. Classroom teachers using this technique almost always see participants respond before they pass five on their second count.[2]

God has much to teach us through those we lead—listen to them!

It's critical that you model patience during your first few storying dialogue sessions in order for your group to become accustomed to sharing openly when you ask questions.

Be Present and Attentive

A big part of storying is caring for people in the process. Give the group your undivided attention. We must believe that what our participants share has meaning for our lives, too. God has much to teach us through those we lead—listen to them! It's easy for us as discussion leaders to get impatient and distracted. We begin thinking about the next question, or we get tired of hearing participants share similar responses. Don't ignore or look past someone when she's sharing. *Be present!* For example, smile expectantly and nod as participants speak. Maintain eye contact. Look relaxed and genuinely interested. Try to never interrupt a participant's response. If we're not engaged in what they're sharing, then the group members will read our body language and begin to feel unheard and unimportant. Henri Nouwen challenges us to work at the art of being present while listening:

> To listen is very hard, because it asks of us so much interior stability that we no longer need to prove ourselves by speeches, arguments, statements, or declarations. True listeners no longer have an inner need to make their presence known. They are free to receive, to welcome, to accept.
>
> Listening is much more than allowing another to talk while waiting for a chance to respond. Listening is paying full attention to others and welcoming them into our very beings. The beauty of listening is that, those who are listened to start feeling accepted, start taking their words more seriously and discovering their own true selves. Listening is a form of spiritual hospitality by which you invite strangers to become friends, to get to know their inner selves more fully, and even to dare to be silent with you.[3]

Help Participants Draw Insights from the Story

After insights are given, ask, "Where did we see that in the story?" This will help the group recall and articulate where they saw it, and it may spark them to remember other occurrences in the stories where something similar happened. This will also encourage participants to look to the story for insights, as well as discourage tangents.

Embrace Perplexity and Mystery

One of the great things about storying is that it sparks our imagination. We begin to envision the stories as reality. I love asking my group, "What do you wonder about from this story? What questions does it bring about?" This brings about all kinds of questions and curiosity. How did the serpent move before it crawled on its belly? This is good! Wondering about biblical events and characters helps us to realize that God is bigger

> Think of your job as creating a safe environment for chaos and a crisis of faith.

and more creative than we thought. Participants will learn and think more for themselves if you leave room for unanswered questions, tension, mystery, and wonder. Think of your job as creating a safe environment for chaos and a crisis of faith.

Encourage Connections to Previous Stories (Not Future Ones)

One of the most powerful parts of the storying experience is seeing people make connections between the stories. Encourage this by asking questions such as, "Where have you seen God do that before in the stories?" While looking backward is good, looking forward is not recommended. It takes away from an intentional investment in the current story.

Keep the Conversation Going

Questions and curiosity drive learning. Once learners believe they have all the answers, they stop asking questions, and they soon stop learning. Become an expert at redirecting questions back to the group, sparking further conversation and wondering. This will create an environment where deep learning can more readily take place. Don't be content with just one answer; ask what others in the group are thinking until several people have had the opportunity to answer.

> Questions and curiosity drive learning.

Here are some ways you can keep the conversation going, adapted from Karen Lee-Thorp's *How to Ask Great Questions*:[4]

> › **Clarifying**—Can you tell me a little bit more?
> › **Question**—Where have we seen this happen before?
> › **Follow-Up**—Why do you think that is?
> › **Bouncing**—That's a great question. Does anyone in the group have any thoughts on that?
> › **Brainstorming**—Let's see how many ideas our group can come up with. . .
> › **Sharing**—I also noticed the connection between. . .
> › **Answering**—In the story the character said. . .
> › **Bringing New Observations**—One thing no one mentioned was. . .

- › **Identifying Themes**—What did we see in this story that we also saw in previous ones?
- › **Summarizing**—So what was one thing that stood out to you from the story?
- › **Prompting**—Who would like to share what they written or drawn?
- › **Restating**—So what you're saying is. . .
- › **Connecting**—What you're saying is connected to what Tom said. . .
- › **Feedback**—How are you feeling about this process so far? What's helpful? What's challenging?
- › **Refocusing**—That's a really interesting thought, but let's get back to the question I asked. . .
- › **Identifying**—How do you think we're like the people in the story? Unlike them?
- › **Applying**—How does this story challenge you personally?

Here are some helpful questions and phrases that I often use (and sometimes overuse):

That's interesting. . .

I wonder that too!

I don't know. I'm not sure.

So you think. . . hmm. . . does anyone else have a thought?

What did the story say about that?

I love your imagination and creativity!

That relates to what _____ said earlier. . .

What part of the story made you think that?

I have heard that. . . what do you think?

Our church teaches. . . what do you think?

Would someone be willing to research that?

I'd love to hear from some of you who haven't shared.

Say the first thing that comes to your mind. . .

Involve Quiet People

When I lead a dialogue, I try to make sure everyone is engaged and sharing observations. If someone isn't responding to the questions, I'll call on him or her. I've noticed that occasionally calling on people who aren't sharing helps build greater attentiveness in the group. But this must be done with tact and sensitivity.

We must keep in mind that quiet participants aren't necessarily disengaged from the discussion. Sometimes those who are a bit more reserved are tracking the discussion and are intellectually active as participants. It's often the quiet participants who share the most profound and deep observations. We must allow space in the dialogue for them to feel safe to share their thoughts. If your group is active and engaged, quiet participants might not feel like as though their input is needed and won't interrupt to be heard.

Some of the following tactics can help engage quieter participants:

› Ask them to share opinions and "wonderings"—something that doesn't call for a correct response. These types of questions are less threatening.

› Make it a point to give them a little extra encouragement when they share.

› Give them outlets to share in smaller groups and through other mediums (art, music, poetry, etc.).

› Provide opportunities for them to write their responses before sharing them out loud.

› Sit next to a quiet (or problematic) participant. Proximity to the leader sometimes draws such participants into dialogue.

Redirect Tangents

Crazy stuff might (and probably will) be said in your storying group. Tangents will fly like bottle rockets. You'll have to be sensitive enough to others—and to God's Spirit—to know when to rein it in. You'll have to be skilled enough to redirect and challenge learners to keep thinking, sharing, and digging for real meaning.

Don't Kill the Discussion[5]

Youth ministry expert Grahame Knox suggests five sure-fire ways to avoid an embarrassing silence:

1. Don't ask questions that can be answered with one word (e.g., Do you agree that God loves you?)

2. Don't ask loaded questions that suggest the answer (e.g., Our bodies are God's temple, so should we smoke?)

3. Don't ask intimidating questions (e.g., If you really loved God, what you would do?)

4. Don't ask embarrassing questions (e.g., What's your most frequent temptation?)

5. Don't try to make people guess the answers you want (e.g., What are the three great truths from this passage?)[5]

I'll add one more: Don't use "Why?" or "Why not?" in your follow-up questions (because they make people feel as though they're defending their answers)]

Discourage Distracting or Inappropriate Questions

Sometimes a participant will ask a question to sidetrack the group, get attention, or just embarrass you. If possible, redirect the group with a new question. If what's asked has created too much distraction, tactfully address what about the question is inappropriate and move on.

Steer away from participants who monopolize the discussion. The best way to avoid monopolizers is to have participants raise their hands—this gives you the option to distribute the responses across the whole group. You can also direct the question to other participants by saying, "I'd love to know what Jenny thinks about this."

If the monopolizer is a serious problem, speak to him or her after group time. Tell the participant that you value his or her participation and need help getting more participants involved in the discussion.

Allow "Communal Correcting" to Take Place

The group will help each other to ensure that key details of the stories are recounted accurately and not missed. When the group corrects people, they're less likely to withdraw from the discussion than they are when a leader corrects them. Correcting just becomes a refining part of the conversation.

Encourage, Encourage, Encourage!

Bible storying, in many ways, is an exercise in affirmation. It is about building confidence in the reality that God stirs, illuminates and teaches through each one of us. What we see and observe and name from the biblical accounts matter. Each time we meet I remind my group members that they will notice things in the Bible story, and they need to share what God illuminates to them. Not only do I believe this, but it also helps create a healthy level of reverence for what each member shares. It inspires them to have faith and listen intently to the story. After participants share, I often acknowledge and genuinely encourage them, saying things like, "That is a great insight" or "Great observation! I've never heard that before," or "That is well said," "That is really making me think," and "Thank you for sharing."

> Bible storying, in many ways, is an exercise in affirmation. It is about building confidence in the reality that God stirs, illuminates and teaches through each one of us.

Share Your Observations

Many have asked me, "Is it okay for me to share my observations if I'm leading the group?" My answer is always, "Yes! But never share first." The hardest part of leading others through storying dialogue is being patient and allowing the process to unfold. Don't try to be the expert—if the group knows you're going to give "the answers," they'll stop sharing.

Pick your spots to share appropriately so they don't squelch the learning process. In groups that I lead, I primarily share only my wonderings and questions from the stories.

Another question I'm asked is, "Should I answer when a participant asks me a question about the Bible?"

Whenever possible, I try not to answer participants' questions directly because it works against efforts to create a participative learning environment.

If I believe someone in the group can answer the question, I redirect it to the group. This not only encourages more participation, but it also implies that peers are a resource for learning.

If I don't know the answer, I tell the group I don't know. If I think that the answer would be helpful and connect to what we are learning, I'll sometimes assign a participant to research it before the next meeting.

If the question is a major tangent but still a good question, I'll try to postpone the answer, saying, "That's a really good question; why don't we talk about that at the end if we have time?" Then I also have the option to just give my response to a few participants.

On rare occasions if a participant asks me for my opinion about a Bible question, and I think it will help the group, I'll share my thoughts. Then I'll try to follow up my thoughts with a question (e.g., "If that's true about Abraham, what do you think that tells us about his relationship with God?")

Doug Pagitt, in his book *Preaching Re-Imagined*, encourages leaders to use provisional statements. In other words, "It seems to me. . . " "As I understand it. . . and so on, in order to create "a culture of openness and invitation. These words make room for the thoughts and experiences of others."[6]

When I've felt the need to share a deeper thought about the story, I try to use provisional statements in the hope that they won't steamroll others and come across as the "right answers."

DIALOGUE GOALS

The goal of a storying dialogue is to encourage participants to share their observations and "wonderings" about the story.

Leading a dialogue requires us to...

> Let go...of the role of expert teacher and embrace the role of co-learner, encourager, and guide.

> Listen...in expectation that God is revealing Godself to and through each person present.

> Trust...that God will work through the process, valuing the experience as much as the knowledge and content.

> Be patient...allowing time to process, room for different opinions, tangents, tension, questions, and wondering.

> Have faith...that God bring to light truth and implications.

Storying dialogue requires a lot of patience, shepherding, encouragement, and practice. After a few stories, participants will get into the rhythm of this process, and they will begin to really listen and think deeply about the story.

BIBLE STORYING IS LIKE FLYING A KITE

Echo the Story is a challenging and rewarding process to lead. It requires us to come alongside our group as a co-learner and facilitator. I compare it to flying a kite, where the imagination and the Spirit of God take the conversation to unexpected places, but the story remains the tether. To lead this well, you need to focus on being fully present with your group, continually affirming and encouraging them, redirecting, connecting ideas, and sparking curiosity and wonder. If you work at developing these skills and sensitivities, you'll create a great environment for you and your group to be *shaped by the story*.

QUESTIONS FOR REFLECTION AND DISCUSSION

› *Who is the best discussion leader you know? What makes this person so great?*

› *What are some of the challenges of leading a storying dialogue?*

› *How is this different than some of the discussion or small-group leader roles you've experienced?*

› *What are some ways you can spark your group's imagination and creativity?*

› *What do you believe it takes to be an effective storying dialogue leader?*

A TRUE STORY ABOUT STORYING

Thank you, thank you for the innovative oral storytelling curriculum outlined in *Shaped by the Story*. Storying provides the structure I need to create a dynamic and engaging atmosphere in my ninth-grade Theology class without losing academic intensity. Every two weeks, I lead an eagerly anticipated storying session. By entering the narratives imaginatively and allowing participants the emotional freedom to wonder about the story, I am able to get the "hook" needed to maintain interest in our intense study of the religious truths and doctrine suggested by the narrative. No matter how far our discussions range during the course of the two weeks, the next story brings us back to the grand narrative and the participants can see how all the pieces fit together. By the end of the course, most participants are surprised to realize that with only a little prompting from the story symbols, they can proudly give a detailed and engaging overview of the important events of scripture.

An additional benefit of storying is that it engages every participant in the course regardless of her previous exposure to the Bible. Some of my participants have had little experience with scripture, while others are extremely well versed in all the important stories. By sharing stories orally, every participant feels as if she is hearing it for the first time and there is excitement and the wonder of discovery that is essential to true connection. Academic differences are bridged, because strong readers as well as those who struggle with comprehension become swept up in the drama, and each participant feels able to respond freely without the fear that she has not understood some aspect of the story correctly. Because my participants come from increasingly secular homes, differentiation has become vital, and storying helps me keeping the playing field level for all the learners in my classroom.

Best of all, storying has helped me transition from a traditional scripture class into the new USCCB bishop's curriculum fairly seamlessly. Both courses have benefitted from the spiritual energy and emotional depth of oral storytelling. Participants share that in either course the true heart of their learning springs from the sacred narratives, and that storying has been the key to discovering God's interest in creating a story in their own lives. The final assignment in my course is for the participants to write their own script about God's action in their life and their response to it, so they can see how their own commitment to discipleship is a vital part of the grand narrative.

Testimonial from Jacque Bischoff, sophomore: "While listening to the Bible stories orally in class, I was able to imagine things I had never recognized in the stories before. I saw things more clearly and I could relate to God on a more personal level. I could experience how people lived and suffered during that time and relate the stories to my own life and anxieties. The stories allowed me to experience God's point of view and how he wants us to experience life with his love and guidance."

Testimonial from Karissa Simon, freshman: "I am glad that we acted out the story [in the Re-Tell portion of storying] because it puts you in the shoes of the character. Even though it was just acting, it didn't make it any easier to 'kill' my son [Isaac]. It made me realize how many sacrifices God made for us."

—JEANNIE STEENBERGE, THEOLOGY INSTRUCTOR FROM SAINT LOUIS, MISSOURI

conclusion

Beginning Your Storying Adventure

Bible storying has changed my life. It has helped me—and many others—to listen to the Scriptures in a new way. I regularly get emails from small group leaders, youth workers, and students who've been transformed by God through Bible storying. Their stories of faith are inspiring and humbling. Here are a couple of responses that have stuck with me:

> My students were immersed in the Scriptures in a way they have never been before. They have a greater understanding of the Story of Stories. They became a part of the Story! This was an opportunity for us to engage in a life-changing experience.
> —DAVID, YOUTH WORKER

> The stories came alive to our students—the more they talked about them, the more they saw different ways they connected to their lives. They were learning for themselves—and this learning sticks! I was right there with the students...the stories came alive for me, too!
> —RACHEL, VOLUNTEER

> I began to see the context of my life within God's story. The Bible's not distant anymore. It's like—whoa!—my life has merged with God's Story. I'm part of what God is doing. I'm a kingdom participant and builder. I realize that community is the most important thing I could give my life to. That's what its all about—a bunch of people getting together to live collectively and individually the life Jesus came to show us.
> —NATALIE, HIGH SCHOOL SENIOR

The Bible can shape our lives in profound ways. When we allow ourselves to be captured by this amazing story, it reveals to us how we were created to live and what role we play in bringing God's love and restoration to the world.

To be shaped by the story requires "a willingness to take a step of faith—to enter the simplicity of the stories to discover the complexity that lies beyond...giving our selves to the story in hope and belief that God will meet us there. It is as Jesus said, 'Unless you become like a child, you shall not enter the kingdom of God.'

It is standing under to understand . . . like a child . . . and to be swept away by God's Story."[1]

Bible storying is an adventure, a journey into the divine mystery and beauty of God. Storying acts as a map to guide us through the Bible toward discovering the amazing power and love of God. This adventure is not easy. Storying is unpredictable, unsettling, and full of wonder and moments of awakening. It moves us into uncharted waters, embarking on a new path of learning that asks a lot from our group and us. The reward of this adventure is great—a community of people transformed by God, ready to change the world.

Together, may we truly be *shaped by the story*.

appendices

APPENDIX A: TWELVE STORY BIBLE OVERVIEW

Used in the resource
Echo the Story: Youth
www.wearesparkhouse.org

	Creation – This story carries us from the God hovering over the dark surface and initiating all life forms through walking with Adam and Eve in harmony in the garden. The centerpiece of the story is about God's remarkable creative power to reform the earth into a place of vibrancy and life.	Genesis 1–3
	Disruption – The story details Adam and Eve's disobedience and consequences. The story moves from Cain murdering Abel to worldwide escalation of evil and a cataclysmic flood. The key identifier is human choice to rebel.	Genesis 3–9
	The Promise – The story details Abraham's calling to trust God's promise that he will be given an amazing new land and a growing family that will become a nation to reflect God's ways to the world. Abraham must trust God through impossible circumstances. A key moment in the story where God promised that Abraham's descendants would be as many as the stars… a vision of promise and hope.	Genesis 12–13; 15–18; 21
	Exodus – This story details Moses's exchange with Pharaoh and the plagues that followed. It ends with the miraculous exodus of the Israelites, guided by a fire/cloud pillar, then crossing the divide in the sea.	Exodus 1–5; 7–15
	Commands – The story details Moses leading the Israelites through the desert and God giving them special instructions for life on the tablets–boundaries providing a clear way to live distinctly better.	Exodus 19–20; 24–25; 31–32; 34; 40
	Judges and Kings – The story details the rise of the Israelites into a nation who struggles in battle with neighboring people. It zeroes in on the triumphs and character challenges of Israel's kings.	Numbers 14; 22; Joshua 11; Judges 2–3; 17; 21; 1 Samuel 8–9; 13–18; 22–23; 26; 31; 2 Samuel 5; 7–8; 11–12; 1 Kings 14

	Exile – The story details the physical and spiritual destruction that Israel encounters while being scattered from their homeland. Prophets speak a message of enduring hope, reclaiming what was lost. A remnant regroups and rebuilds a modest temple, but they still long to be free and hang on to the promise that they will again have their own king and kingdom.	1 Kings 3–5; 8–14; 2 Kings 17; 24–25; 2 Chronicles 7; 36; Amos 3–5; 7; Jeremiah 18; 23; 29; 31; Ezekiel 36; Ezra 1–2; Nehemiah 4; 6
	God-with-us – The story details the birth of Jesus and the reactions of those who God visits with this good news. Wise men follow a star to find the new king. The story is about a new beginning, an in-breaking of the divine into humanity, a new hope.	Luke 1–3; Matthew 1–3; Mark 1; John 1
	Miracles – The stories highlighted in this lesson are Jesus's calming of the storm and lowering of the paralytic into the crowded house. It centers on the amazing power of Jesus and people's reaction to his remarkable healings and calming of the storm.	Matthew 8–9; Mark 2; 4; Luke 4–5; John 5
	Kingdom – The scenes detailed in this story are Jesus's teachings and parables about God's kingdom and the sermon on the mount. The story is about the alternative kingdom that Jesus paints through parables that stands in contrast to the corruption of the religious and political systems of the day.	Matthew 5; 12–13; 18; 20; 22; Mark 2;10; Luke 11; 13–14; 17
	Death-to-life – The story details Jesus's last supper, arrest and crucifixion. It ends with the initial sightings of and joyful reactions to the resurrected Jesus. The story embodies the rising of new life, potential and a new era.	Matthew 26–28; Luke 19; 22–24; John 11; 15
	The Church – This is the story of the formation of the church and their close community. It details the Acts 2 events of speaking in other languages but the main focus is on this being the beginning of our story... us living out the story as the church and bringing healing to the world. This story speaks of the community of God's family extending the compassionate work of Jesus. It is about potential, unity and family.	Acts 1–2

APPENDIX B: SAMPLE SCRIPTURE

For use with worksheets in appendices C and D

Genesis 4

NEW REVISED STANDARD VERSION (NRSV)

1 Now the man knew his wife Eve, and she conceived and bore Cain, saying, "I have produced a man with the help of the Lord." 2 Next she bore his brother Abel. Now Abel was a keeper of sheep, and Cain a tiller of the ground. 3 In the course of time Cain brought to the Lord an offering of the fruit of the ground, 4 and Abel for his part brought of the firstlings of his flock, their fat portions. And the Lord had regard for Abel and his offering, 5 but for Cain and his offering he had no regard. So Cain was very angry, and his countenance fell. 6 The Lord said to Cain, "Why are you angry, and why has your countenance fallen? 7 If you do well, will you not be accepted? And if you do not do well, sin is lurking at the door; its desire is for you, but you must master it."

8 Cain said to his brother Abel, "Let us go out to the field." And when they were in the field, Cain rose up against his brother Abel, and killed him. 9 Then the Lord said to Cain, "Where is your brother Abel?" He said, "I do not know; am I my brother's keeper?" 10 And the Lord said, "What have you done? Listen; your brother's blood is crying out to me from the ground! 11 And now you are cursed from the ground, which has opened its mouth to receive your brother's blood from your hand. 12 When you till the ground, it will no longer yield to you its strength; you will be a fugitive and a wanderer on the earth." 13 Cain said to the Lord, "My punishment is greater than I can bear! 14 Today you have driven me away from the soil, and I shall be hidden from your face; I shall be a fugitive and a wanderer on the earth, and anyone who meets me may kill me." 15 Then the Lord said to him, "Not so! Whoever kills Cain will suffer a sevenfold vengeance." And the Lord put a mark on Cain, so that no one who came upon him would kill him. 16 Then Cain went away from the presence of the Lord, and settled in the land of Nod, east of Eden.

APPENDIX C: DEVELOPING A BIBLE STORYING NARRATIVE WORKSHEET

1. Read through chapter 10: Developing Bible Storying in this book to provide more context and direction in stitching together and smoothing over a narrative for Bible storying.

2. This is not intended to be a comprehensive process, but rather to give you a sense of some of the steps involved in crafting your own Bible storying narratives. Have fun!

3. To complete this activity, you will need to select a section of scripture that tells a Bible story. We have included the scripture from Genesis 4 (Cain and Abel) in appendix C as an option.

FIRST READING

Read the passage of Scripture you have selected using your imagination. Connect with your senses as you consider yourself an eyewitness to the events described. Picture the events in your mind, imagining the sounds, tastes, scents, and colors. *Slow down and enjoy this reading!* Write down parts of the story that stand out to you here:

APPENDIX C — CONTINUED...

STORY MAPPING

Draw a story map like the example below. Identify the main events, conflict points, climax, resolution, and conclusion of the story on your chart. You may want to sketch this out with pencil or on a separate piece of paper so you can make adjustments.

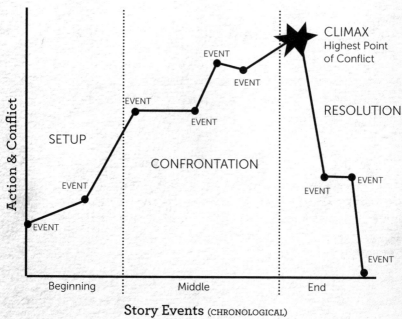

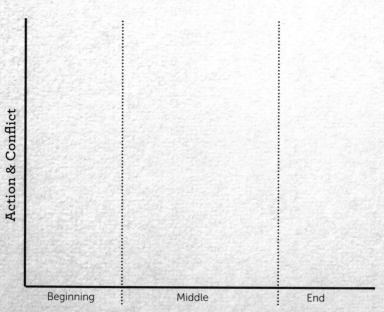

If your story map shows multiple high peaks and climax points, you might be selecting too large of a chunk of Scripture to tell. It might need to be split into two story sessions or the details of your narrative will need to be simplified. Ask yourself, "What are the essential events that communicate this story?"

Stitching Together a Story

Hopefully your story map helped you to determine the key action in the story. Now you must shorten the length of the story.

1. Cut and paste the Scripture into a word processing document or print it out on paper (www.biblegateway.com is an easy-to-use online Bible).

2. Mark sections that you would *leave out* for your tellable narrative.

3. A good rule of thumb is to not to introduce more than 5 names of people or places in the story. Limit proper nouns, geographic locations, and technical details. Most of this was immediately relevant to the original hearers, but would take a lot of time for you to build context and significance for your group.

I know this part feels a little strange, as though you are editing scripture. But keep in mind your job is to give people a snapshot they can take with them. This snapshot will not only help them see the whole of the biblical story, it will ignite curiosity to want to learn and read more about the story.

Smoothing Over Wording

As you went through the task of cutting out segments of the narrative, you probably noticed parts you wanted to leave but are still a bit awkward to tell as a story.

Get out a blank sheet of paper and carefully rewrite the entire Scripture segment, smoothing over the language to make it more tellable. This is not an attempt to modernize the text, but rather make it more accessible and clear.

NOTE: for a more detailed process of how to develop Bible storying narratives, see chapter 10 of this book.

APPENDIX D: DEVELOPING BIBLE STORYING QUESTIONS

Brainstorm storying questions below using the Bible passage provided in appendix B or another Bible story of your choice.

For more details about Bible Storying Questions read chapters 11: The Bible Storying Process, and chapter 12 Leading an Effective Dialogue.

WONDERING QUESTIONS (imaginative / divergent)

Look to spark imaginative responses with open-ended sensory questions. For example, *"How would you have felt if you were in the boat with Jesus during the storm?"*

1.

2.

REMEMBERING QUESTIONS (reflective / convergent)

When asking remembering questions, you're looking for participants to put what they remember into words. For example: *"What did God create in this story?" Anything else?..."*

1.

2.

NOTE: If my group remembers most of the details of the story during the retelling, I'm apt to skip over the remembering questions.

INTEGRATING QUESTIONS (interpretive / divergent)

Integrating questions are intended to help participants to verbalize patterns, synthesize observations, and weave together meaning. For example: *"What was God like in this story?"*

1.

2.

CONNECTING QUESTIONS (decisive / convergent)

Connecting questions stir participants to think about how the story connects to their own lives. For example: *"What do you believe it means to be created in the image of God?"*

1.

2.

APPENDIX E: CREATING AN ENVIRONMENT FOR BIBLE STORYING

The purpose of storying is to *create an environment that invites God to shape us through the biblical story.* How do we create that environment? It is not easy. We must slow down and listen. It takes patience, persistent encouragement, and reframing. Most of all, it takes reliance on God's Spirit to teach and guide us, revealing to us truth and new meaning.

For more on creating an environment for Bible sorying, read chapter 10 Developing Bible Storying.

Brainstorm some ways you can create an environment for storying in your ministry:

Ideas for your meeting room or space:

Ideas to help ready your leaders:

Ideas to help ready your group:

APPENDIX F: PROVIDING CREATIVE OPTIONS

Provide creative and reflective options during the CAPTURE and REMIX parts of Bible Storying. These segments are intended to help participants engage with the story in deeper ways. You may want to set up stations based on the ways people learn.

Allowing choice to creatively respond to the story empowers learning. Storying should not be overly concerned with recounting details of the story, but with seeing the story through each other's eyes and building shared meaning. Brainstorm some creative and reflective options that you could provide for your group, based on these ways of learning:

VISUAL LEARNERS

LITERARY LEARNERS

HANDS-ON LEARNERS

AUDITORY LEARNERS

For more detail on the segments of Bible storying, read chapter 11 The Bible Storying Process. Also, read chapter 9 Storying and Learning to find out more about how storying connects with multiple learning styles.

APPENDIX G: SIMPLE BIBLE STORYING SESSION

CREATION: SESSION OVERVIEW

1. **REWIND the story**
    A brief introduction of the power of story and the process of storying. In subsequent sessions this time is used to review previous stories told.

2. **PREPARE for the story**
    The leader will share a scripted segment that helps to create a reflective environment and encourage imaginative listening.

3. **IMAGINE the story**
    The leader will now verbally tell this session's Bible story. A carefully crafted narrative script of the story is provided.

SUPPLIES

- Blank paper or sketch pads for each participant.

- Markers, colored pencils, and pens for participants.]

4. **CAPTURE what you notice**
    The leader will then ask someone of an opposite gender to do a second telling of the story. During this telling, participants will capture aspects of the story that stood out to them through journaling, creative writing, or art.

5. **CONNECT to your story**
    Finally, the leader will guide a group dialogue asking participants to share their observations and insights from the story. A set of intentional questions is provided in this Leader Guide.

ABOUT THIS SIMPLIFIED SESSION:

This is the BASIC Echo the Story process I have used for years, and continue to use in my workshops.

Sparkhouse's Echo the Story: Youth resource uses an expanded process that includes a shortened CAPTURE segment and an additional segment called **REMIX the story**. Additional elements are also included with the Echo the Story: Youth resources like the *Story So Far* video recap and a participant *Sketch Journal*. The Sketch Journal includes activities to help your group retell (remix) the story in their own way, using their own preferred learning style.

To learn more about this new resource, go to
www.echo.wearesparkhouse.org.

APPENDIX G — CONTINUED...

REWIND THE STORY

LEADER SAYS:

Take a moment in quiet and think about a favorite story–it could be from a movie, a novel, or a story told to you.

> **CUE:** pause for 20 seconds.

Now, turn to someone next to you and share a one minute version of that story and why you think it is a good story.

> **CUE:** after 2 minutes of sharing, ask a few people to share with the group. *Why do you think we connect so well with stories?*

> **CUE:** get a few responses.

Good stories capture our imaginations. . . they draw us in. We begin to feel what the characters feel. . . their pain becomes our pain ... their victory becomes our victory. Without us realizing it, a story can get under our skin, influence our thoughts, and stir our emotions.

We don't often think of it this way, but the Bible is over 70 percent narrative, comprised of hundreds of stories that fit together to tell one really big, inter-connected story. The Bible is God's amazing story of rescuing and restoring all of life to its very best.

Right now, we're going to try a new approach to learning from the Bible called "storying." This unique approach is rooted in the ancient Hebrew way of learning through storytelling, careful observation, and dialogue.

The Bible is filled with wild stories that recount extraordinary events that seem unbelievable to our modern minds. Rather than dismiss them as fairy tales, we must come to these stories in a different way...beyond just rational deductions...and use our intuition and wonder, asking, *"What would it have been like to be there? What deep meaning can be found in this story?"*

As you listen carefully and with your imagination, God will bring to light a part of the story. . . an image, a connection. . . something that you have never seen before. Following the story you will have a chance to share that with us!

PREPARE FOR THE STORY

SEVENTY FACES OF TORAH

Leader Says: I want to share a helpful way we can look at the Bible.

Even though this is written like a script, please personalize the "Leader Says" parts.

For nearly a thousand years, Jewish rabbis have passed on a special way of looking at Scripture. They call it the *Seventy Faces of Torah*—the Torah being the first five books of the Bible. This phrase comes from comparing Scripture to a beautiful diamond with seventy sides or faces.

Imagine holding up a diamond and slowly turning it, allowing light to reflect further detail, beauty, depth, and brilliance off of its many sides.

As the ancient Jewish people listened and looked deeply into the Scriptures, they anticipated that each person would see something unique reflected back, illuminated from the same source of light—*God's Spirit*.

My challenge to us is to choose now to turn the diamond of Scripture, and look deeply within the story—expecting God to illuminate something new to each one of us.

And when you see something in the story—something simple, or beautiful, or profound—I hope you will share it with the group! Each reflection can teach us something new.

Let's take a moment and get ready for imaginative listening. Imagine the story playing in your mind like a movie. Put yourself in the story and try to sense what is going on.

Right now, do what helps you to concentrate the best. That could mean closing your eyes (stay awake!), or focusing on the image on the screen.

Are you ready? Take a moment in silence to take a deep breath, slow down, and clear your mind. Whisper a prayer asking God to show you something meaningful in this story.

› **CUE:** After fifteen to twenty-seconds of quiet, begin narrating the story.

APPENDIX G — CONTINUED...

IMAGINE THE STORY

Leader Narrates:

SCENE ONE: Beginnings

Scene One of this story, from Genesis 1, was told by the ancient Israelites for many generations and it begins like this:

The Creator . . .

a great and mysterious being called God—

formed the Earth and the heavens and above.

While the Earth was still shapeless, dark, and empty,

God hovered over the waters.

As God spoke, creation began taking shape.

God made light. . . and pushed back the darkness.

God separated the sky from the oceans and seas . . .

and gathered the waters, allowing dry land to appear.

God made plants, flowers, and trees grow . . .

all with seeds in them so they could reproduce themselves.

God created the sun, the moon, and the stars . . .

setting the days, months, and seasons into motion.

God formed all kinds of creatures . . . fish that swim in the seas,

birds that fly through the air, and wild animals that run and crawl across the land.

The Earth was filled with extraordinary life.

Looking at this creation, God said, *"This is good!"*

Then God created another kind of creature: *human beings.*

God created both men and women to reflect God's own image.

And God said to the humans, *"Continue my creative work.*

Start a family, and take care of all living things." [pause]

Looking at all of this wonderful creation, God said, *"This is very good!"*

Then God rested . . . and set aside a day in each week for humans to rest and enjoy being with God. [a] [pause]

SCENE TWO: First Humans

Scene Two, from Genesis 2, gives a more detailed view of the creation of human beings. It begins like this:

While all the plants and trees were still just seeds in the earth, God caused water to mist from the ground and start their growth. [pause]

Then God used dirt from the Earth to form the first human.

When God breathed breath into the human's nostrils, suddenly he came to life!

He would be known as Adam, *meaning from the ground;* also meaning human being.

God placed this human in a garden filled with beautiful plants and delicious fruit.

Sparkling rivers flowed through the center of this garden.

God gave the human great responsibility: to work in the garden and care for all living things. God even brought each kind of animal right to Adam so he could give them names.

In the middle of this garden stood two special trees—the *Tree of Life* and the *Tree of Knowing Good and Evil.* God told Adam, *"Enjoy fruit from any tree—except for one. If you eat fruit from the Tree of Knowing Good and Evil, you will die."* [pause]

Soon God said to Adam, *"It's not good for you to be alone.*

I will make a partner that is just right for you!"

So God caused Adam to fall into a deep sleep, removed one of his sides,

and filled in the place it had been taken from.

God used Adam's side to form the first woman.

APPENDIX G — CONTINUED...

When God brought her to Adam, Adam shouted, *"At last!"*

Adam would soon call his new companion Eve, meaning *giver of life.*[b]

Adam and Eve were joined together as one.

Although they were naked, they never felt ashamed. [pause]

 And God would come and walk with them in the cool of the day.[c]

Isaiah 58:13-14   (b) Genesis 3:20   (c) Genesis 3:8a

CAPTURE WHAT YOU NOTICE

MOMENT OF REFLECTION

Leader Says:

Take a quiet moment to close your eyes and let the story replay in your mind like a movie. Don't rush this. Allow yourself to explore the story again. Pay attention to what you see and sense, and the parts of the story that stand out to you.

› **CUE:** After twenty seconds of quiet, continue.

CAPTURE WHAT YOU NOTICE

Leader Says:

We are going to listen to the story again, this time with a different voice telling it. During this telling of the story, you have some option to capture what you are seeing in the story. So, right now you may choose to:

SKETCH scenes that stood out to you...
Draw the story as you see it. This could be a picture of a scene, or several on a page, like a storyboard.

WRITE about what stood out to you...
Put yourself in this story. Write about what you see. Journal, write a poem, a song, a spoken word piece, or a short story.

LISTEN for what stands out to you...
Listen carefully with your imagination (don't fall asleep!). Put yourself in this story. Think about what stands out to you and how you will share it during our upcoming dialogue time.

Your thoughts, words, sketches and creativity are important here. Pay attention to what stands out to you from the story.

› **CUE:** For this second telling, use a storyteller of an opposite gender from your first telling. Different voices help people to listen with fresh ears.

Leader Says: [After the second telling] Take another minute or two to finish capturing your thoughts, then we'll share with each other.

› **CUE:** After about two minutes, go to the next section.

CONNECT TO YOUR STORY

Leader Says:
I am excited to hear what you saw and sensed in this story! I'm not looking for specific answers; it's your observations that have meaning. Who'd like to share?

* What stood out to you from this story?

* What did this story make you wonder about?

› **LEADER:** *Do not* give answers to participants wonderings and questions. In fact, share an example of what you are wondering about the story

* What were the relationships like in the story?

    – In what part(s) of the story did you notice this?

    – What did Adam say when he first saw Eve?

* Why do you think God gave humans responsibilities?

    – What responsibilities were given to the humans?

    – What might this show us about God?

APPENDIX G — CONTINUED...

- How might work have been different from what it is now?

* How might this story give us a glimpse of our true identities?

* Share the *first* thing that comes to your mind when I ask this question: What do you notice about *God* in this story?

- Where in the story did you see this?

FINAL QUESTION: Take a moment in quiet and think about this last question:

* What does it mean for *you* (personally) to be created in God's image?

› **CUE:** After about fifteen seconds of quiet, ask *a few* participants to share. Encourage participants to personalize their ideas using *"I"* and *"me"* instead of *"you"* and *"we"* language. This helps keep participants from being overly general or preachy.

› **CUE:** To close this session, ask someone to pray.

APPENDIX H: BIBLE STORYING IN AFRICA BY JOHN WITTE

Introduction

John Witte is the person who first introduced me to Bible storying. He inspired and challenged me to pursue this powerful approach to the Scriptures within a North American context. The following story was transcribed from an interview I did with John in April 2008 for www.echothestory.com.—*Michael Novelli*

John's Story on Storying:

My ministry training was a typical seminary education, based on exegesis of the text. I loved that stuff and I still do—it really has formed me in a lot of ways.

In 1990, when my family moved to Kenya, I did a lot of preaching to youth groups and larger churches. People there seemed to respond well to this expository type of preaching, but after some time, I realized that only a few of them could reproduce it. I could show off in front of them, in a sense, and it made me feel good, but it wasn't impacting their lives in terms of them being able to take any of it into ministry themselves.

In 1991, I was introduced to chronological Bible storying by Dr. Jim Slack, a member of our missions board. Dr. Slack was traveling around the world introducing missionaries to this method of teaching people the Scriptures through story and dialogue. When I first heard about this method, I was pretty biased against it because of my love for exegesis and propositional teaching.

I tried storying a few times, and found that the African people responded well to this. In a two-day meeting with the Mossai on the Kenya—Tanzania border, I told about twenty-five stories in Ke-Swahelia and they translated them into Ke-Mossai or Ke-Mo. Even though I was really lousy at it, they loved it!

In spite of some of my positive experiences, I seemed to always return to my expository ways of preaching. It wasn't until years later in Kesumo that I made the conscious decision to communicate using storying and oral strategies appropriate in the African context.

APPENDIX H — CONTINUED...

I realized I must take what I'd learned in seminary and ministry and bend it like a sapling toward the people in order to serve and reach them. I had to learn how to communicate in a whole new way, and to redefine my whole approach—communication became a way to serve to the people I lived among.

I really was pretty bad at storying to begin with, but I kept working hard at it. After some time, a neat thing happened; not only were the stories well received in African settings, but also in the stateside churches when I came back home. I would travel and tell people of how storying was working overseas, then lead them through Bible narratives. People just loved it.

After seeing how people in completely different cultures and continents connected with storying, I was completely convinced that this was the better way, the preferred way to communicate our Christian and biblically-based message to people.

The best experience I had with using oral strategies—storying, dance, drama, and music—was with the Karamojong in northeast Uganda, specifically with the Dodoth. In 2003 when I began working with them, I had four years of experience with storying full-time, and I wanted to apply it in that setting.

The Dodoth are what you might picture tribal African people to be: very isolated and quite proud of their culture. They are pastoralists, a cattle-based culture. Because of the civil war in Sudan, many of them had AK-47 weapons and were constantly raiding one another for cattle. You needed cattle to acquire more wives, and the more wives and the more sons from those wives you had was the way you showed power, wealth, and manhood in that culture.

When I began storying with them, I worked hard at making the stories simpler so they would be more accessible. I also sought out those in the tribe who were very gifted in Karamojong music and dance. They are a culture that is centered around music and dance—that is the way they enjoy life and express joy. Every night they have the potential to be raided for cattle, so the men stay up around the campfire until 2:00 a.m., when it would be too late for intruders to steal and drive their cattle back before daybreak. They live a harsh life, where no one goes out after dark because it is so dangerous. So music and dance are an incredible release for these people.

After I would teach them the biblical narratives, they would put the stories to their own music. Then we would go to different villages nearby and lead the people in storying, and one of the locals would teach the songs for the stories we shared. They already recognized the music and instantly embraced this approach. In twenty or thirty minutes, they were ready to perform the songs they just heard! I also added drama to the storying process with the Karamojong from time to time, and they really liked it! For oral people, drama is a form of interpretation—when they see the story dramatized they have to think through it again and process what really happened. I could tell by the way the people in this region were responding that they felt like, "I can do this, I can be involved in this story and give this away to others."

We did not build any structures or church buildings; we would just sit on rock outcroppings near the village, telling stories, singing, and dancing. These outcroppings were strategic locations providing a place to hide behind rocks and shoot at potential intruders.

We got lots of invitations from other tribes, so we would walk all over the region sharing songs and dramas to introduce people to the story. Song and dance was a like a wave coming in off the ocean with storying coming in behind it to shore it up.

In the south Sudan we also did storying among the Jure—a people who are perhaps more primitive than the Karamojong. The men wear leather loincloths and the women cover themselves with green leaves with a black tail hanging down the back.

We were working with an existing Bible school there, helping train up indigenous leaders. Most of the students were unable to read. One day we got into a discussion with the students about how we can take God's message to other people. The students immediately

APPENDIX H — CONTINUED...

started chiming in, "You teach us differently than our teachers do. When you teach us, we really understand it."

I responded, "Don't judge your teachers too harshly; they are trying and doing the best they know how to do." I said this because I knew they were being taught through Western classroom models focused on proposition and systematic theology, of which I had done years of that kind of teaching in Kenya.

Some of the students continued, "When we were on break we went home and sang the songs and danced, and these little old women came around and joined us. (In their culture they would dance by moving their feet back and forth while they quickly clapped their hands.) These old women loved it—as long as we would sing and dance they would stay around—when we stopped they would leave. Later on these old woman came back and said to us, "Those are really good songs; what do those songs mean?"

So we told them the stories of what those songs mean. When we finished, the old women said to us, "For the first time in our lives, now we understand what the Bible means."

I have goose bumps thinking about this. When I heard the students share this story, I realized that storying and oral teaching methods were not just theory. These were the most under-resourced, under-cared for, forgotten people in the middle of nowhere. They had little or no access to Westernization or Scripture, and now they were saying, "Aha, now we get it."

APPENDIX I: RECOMMENDED BIBLE STORYING RESOURCES

BIBLE STORIES AND OVERVIEWS

A Walk through the Bible
Leslie Newbigin (Vancouver, BC: Regent College Publishing, 1999)

God's Big Picture: Tracing the Storyline of the Bible
Vaughan Roberts (Downers Grove, IL: Inter-Varsity Press, 2002)

God's EPIC Adventure:
Changing Our Culture by the Story We Live and Tell
Winn Griffin (Woodinville, WA: Harmon Press, 2007)

GodStories: New Narratives from Sacred Texts
H. Stephen Shoemaker (Valley Forge, PA: Judson Press, 1998)

Telling God's Story: The Biblical Narrative from Beginning to End
Preben Vang and Terry Carter
(Nashville, TN: Broadman & Holman, 2006)

The Big Story: What Actually Happens in the Bible
Nick Page (Carlisle, UK: Authentic Media, 2007)

The True Story of the Whole World:
Finding Your Place in the Biblical Story
Craig Bartholomew & Michael Goheen
(Grand Rapids, MI: Faith Alive, 2004)

The Story of God, The Story of Us:
Getting Lost and Found in the Bible
Swan Gladding (Downers Grove, IL: IVP, 2010)

The Narrated Bible in Chronological Order
F. Lagard Smith (Eugene, OR: Harvest House, 1984)

The Story, NIV:
The Bible as One Continuing Story of God and His People
31 Bible narratives (Grand Rapids, MI: Zondervan, 2011)

The Storyteller's Companion to the Bible
Commentary Series – several volumes available
(Nashville, TN: Abingdon Press, 1984-2001

APPENDIX I — CONTINUED...

BIBLE STORYTELLING / NARRATIVE THEOLOGY

Story Journey: An Invitation to the Gospel as Storytelling
Thomas E. Boomershine (Nashville, TN: Abingdon Press, 1988)

Tell Me a Story: The Life-Shaping Power of Our Stories
Daniel Taylor (St. Paul, MN: Bog Walk Press, 2001)

The Art of Biblical Narrative
Robert Alter (Cambridge, MA: Basic Books, 1981)

The God-Hungry Imagination: The Art of Storytelling for Postmodern Youth Ministry
Sarah Arthur (Nashville, TN: Upper Room Books, 2007)

Thinking in Story: Preaching in a Post-Literate Age
Richard A. Jensen, (Lima, OH: CSS Publishing, 1995)

To Be Told: God Invites You to Co-Author Your Future
Dan Allender (Colorado Springs, CO: WaterBrook Press, 2006)

How to Ask Great Questions: Guide Your Group to Discovery with These Proven Techniques
Karen Lee-Thorp (Colorado Springs, CO: NavPress, 1998)

The Art of Storytelling: Easy Steps to Presenting an Unforgettable Story
John Walsh (Chicago, Moody Press, 2003)

The Storyteller's Start-Up Book: Finding, Learning, Performing and Using Folktales
Margaret Read MacDonald (Little Rock, AR: August House, 1993)

The Story of God: A Narrative Theology
Michael Lodahl (Kansas City, MO: Beacon Hill, 2008)

ON THE WEB:

Christian Storytelling Network
www.christianstorytelling.com

Chronological Bible Storying
www.oralitystrategies.org

Echo the Story
www.echo.wearesparkhouse.org

Imago – events, design and media
www.imagocommunity.com

International Orality Network
www.oralbible.com

Lego Bible Stories - meant for adults
www.thebricktestament.com

Merge High School Event
www.mergeevent.com

Network of Biblical Storytellers
www.nbsint.org

PBS Storytellers
www.pbs.org/circleofstories

Storytelling Training by John Walsh
www.bibletelling.com

ENDNOTES

CHAPTER FIVE

1   1 Kings 19:11-13 (New Living Translation).

2   Scottie May, "Maria Montessori," Talbot School of Theology, accessed May 17, 2013, http://www2.talbot.edu/ce20/educators/view.cfm?n=maria_montessori.

3   Maria Montessori, *The Child in the Church: Essays on the Religious Education of Children and the Training of Character*, ed. E. M. Standing, (St. Paul: Catechetical Guild, 1965), 56.

4   May, "Maria Montessori."

5   Ron Miller, "Nourishing the Spiritual Embryo: The Educational Vision of Maria Montessori," Paths in Learning, 2002, http://www.pathsoflearning.net/articles_Montessori.pdf. (accessed July 11, 2013).

6   Mario Montessori, Jr., *Education for Human Development: Understanding Montessori* (Offord, UK: ABC-CLIO, 1992), 4.

7   Maria Montessori, *The Montessori Method*, trans. Anne Everett George, (New York: Frederick A. Stokes,,1912), 371.

8   Mario Montessori, Jr., *Education for Human Development: Understanding Montessori*. (Oxford, UK: ABC-CLIO, 1992), 25.

9   Ibid., 7.

10   Catherine Stonehouse and Scottie May, *Listening to Children on the Spiritual Journey: Guidance for Those Who Teach and Nurture*, (Grand Rapids, MI: Baker Academic, 2010), 6.

11   Ibid., 6.

12   Ibid., 7.

13   Ibid., 7.

CHAPTER SIX

1   Christina Baldwin, *StoryCatcher: Making Sense of our Lives Through the Power and Practice of Story.* (Novato, CA: New World Library; 2007), 77.

2   Eugene Peterson, *Christ Plays in Ten Thousand Places: A Conversation in Spiritual Theology* (Grand Rapids, MI: Eerdmans, 2005), 13.

3   Jeremy Hsu, "The Secrets to Storytelling: Why We Love a Good Yarn," *Scientific American*, September 18, 2008, http://www.scientificamerican.com/article.cfm?id=the-secrets-of-storytelling.

4   Ibid.

5   Paul Zak, "The Future of Storytelling," February 19, 2013, YouTube video, 05:57, http://youtu.be/DHeqQAKHh3M.

6   Tony Buzan and Barry Buzan, *The Mind Map Book: How to Use Radiant Thinking to Maximize Your Brain's Untapped Potential.* (New York: Penguin Books, 1993), 53.

7   Robert Ornstein, "'Teaching-Stories' and the Brain," Library of Congress lecture, Nov. 1, 2002, http://www.loc.gov/today/pr/2002/02-147.html.

ENDNOTES

8   Linda Fredericks, "Developing Literacy Skills through Storytelling," Corporation for National and Community Service, 1997, https://www.nationalserviceresources.org/literacy-storytelling.

9   Teresa Méndez, "'Hamlet' Too Hard? Try a Comic Book," *Christian Science Monitor*, October 12, 2004, http://www.csmonitor.com/2004/1012/p11s01-legn.html.

10   Ibid.

11   Kendall F Haven, *Story Proof: The Science Behind the Starling Power of Story.* (Westpoint, CT: Libraries Unlimited, 2007), 9.

12   Baldwin, *StoryCatcher,* 77.

13   Sherrelle Walker, "Using Stories to Teach: How Narrative Structure Helps Students Learn," The Science of Learning (blog), June 14, 2012, http://www.scilearn.com/blog/using-stories-to-teach.php.

14   Robert H. Frank, "Students Discover Economics in Its Natural State," *The New York Times*, September 29, 2005, http://www.nytimes.com/2005/09/29/business/29scene.

15   Haven, *Story Proof,* 44-45.

16   Ibid., vii.

17   Lewis Mehl-Madrona, *Coyote Wisdom: The Power of Story in Healing*, (Rochester, VT: Bear & Company, 2005), 152.

18   Haven, *Story Proof,* 13.

19   Ibid., *Story Proof*, 103.

20   James A Feehan, *Preaching Stories* (Leonminster, UK, Gracewing Publishing, 1989), 19.

CHAPTER SEVEN

1   Jen Wise, "Why Reading the Bible as a Story Matters," Brad Nelson (blog), March 2, 2012, http://bleedingoutloud.com/2012/03/02/jen-wise-why-reading-the-bible-as-a-story-matters.

2   Andrea Phillips, "Stories are the Engine That Drives Culture–And Changes It," GOOD, December 18, 2012, http://www.good.is/posts/stories-are-the-engine-that-drives-culture-and-changes-it.

3   Ibid.

4   Brian Swimme, *The Hidden Heart of the Cosmos: Humanity and the New Story.* (Maryknoll, NY: Orbis Books, 1996), 13-17.

5   Montessori, *Education for Human Development,* 82.

6   Phillip Gang, *Rethinking Education.* (Christchurch, New Zealand: Dagaz Press, 1989), 26.

7   H. Stephen Shoemaker, *Godstories: New Narratives from Sacred Texts* (Valley Forge, PA: Judson Press, 1998), xix.

8   George Barna, *The Second Coming of the Church: A Blueprint for Survival* (Nashville, TN.: Thomas Nelson, 1998), 122.

ENDNOTES

9   Ivy Beckwith , *Formational Children's Ministry: Shaping Children Using Story, Ritual and Relationship* (Grand Rapids, MI: Baker Books, 2010), 25.

10   Ibid., 30.

11   George Barna, "Barna Studies the Research, Offers a Year-in-Review Perspective," Barna Group, December 18, 2009, http://www.barna.org/barna-update/article/12-faithspirituality/325-barna-studies-the-research-offers-a-year-in-review-perspective.

12   Beckwith, *Formational Children's Ministry*, 26.

13   Barbara Horkoff Mutch, "Shaped by the Story: Narrative, Formation, and the Word," Conversations: A Forum for Authentic Transformation, Spring 2005 Vol. 3.1, http://www.onelifemaps.com/wp-content/uploads/2013/03/F4I_V2-Shaped-by-the-story.pdf.

14   Eugene H. Peterson, *The Message Remix: Introduction to the Book of Jonah* (Colorado Springs: NavPress, 2006), 1352.

15   Richard A. Jensen, *Thinking in Story: Preaching in a Post-literate Age* (Lima, Ohio: CSS Publishing, 1993), 9.

16   Colin Harbinson, "Restoring the Arts to the Church: The Role of Creativity in the Expression of Truth," *Lausanne World Pulse Magazine*, July 2006, http://www.lausanneworldpulse.com/themedarticles.php/409/07-2006.

17   Scot McKnight, "Stories on the Story," Ancient Evangelical Future Conference, October 2007, http://desertpastor.typepad.com/paradoxology/files/McNight_Wiki_Story_short.mp3.

18   Harbinson, "Restoring the Arts to the Church," 2006.

19   Jensen, *Thinking in Story*, 9.

20   Walter Brueggemann, *Finally Comes the Poet: Daring Speech for Proclamation* (Minneapolis: Augsburg Fortress, 1989), 109-110.

21   Kenton L. Sparks, *Sacred Word, Broken Word: Biblical Authority and the Dark Side of Scripture* (Grand Rapids, MI: Wm. B. Eerdmans Publishing, 2012) (Kindle 1055-1056).

22   David Fitch, "The Myth of Expository Preaching (Part 2): Proclamation That Inspires the Imagination," Out of Ur (*Christianity Today* blog), July 25, 2006, http://blog.christianitytoday.com/outofur/archives/2006/07/the_myth_of_exp_1.html.

23   Marcus Borg, *Reading the Bible Again for the First Time*, (New York: Harper Collins, 2001), 31.

CHAPTER EIGHT

1   Shoemaker, *Godstories*, xxiv.

2   Thomas E. Boomershine, *Story Journey: An Invitation to the Gospel as Storytelling* (Nashville, TN: Abingdon Press, 1988), 141.

3   Peter Pitzele, "What Is Midrash?" *Living Text*, no. 1, 2-3, 1997, http://www.icmidrash.org.

4   Stephen M. Wylen, *The Seventy Faces of Torah: The Jewish Way of Reading the Sacred Scriptures* (Mahwah, NJ: Paulist, 2005), 62.

ENDNOTES

5   John J. Parsons, "Seventy Faces of Torah: A Brief Overview of Exegesis," http://www.hebrew4christians.com/Articles/Seventy_Faces/70Faces.pdf.

6   Shoemaker, *Godstories*, xxiv.

7   Parsons, "Seventy Faces of Torah."

8   Wylen, *The Seventy Faces of Torah,* 63.

9   Ibid., 70.

10   C. S. Lewis, Bruce L. Edwards, *C.S. Lewis: Life, Works and Legacy,* 4 vol. (Westport, CT: Praeger Publishers, 2007), 237.

11   Sarah Arthur, *The God-Hungry Imagination: The Art of Storytelling for Postmodern Youth Ministry* (Nashville, TN: Upper Room, 2007), 49, 53.

12   Mark Miller, *Experiential Storytelling: (Re) Discovering Narrative to Communicate God's Message* (Grand Rapids, MI: Zondervan/Youth Specialties, 2003), 24.

CHAPTER NINE

1   Peter Honey and Alan Mumford, *The Manual of Learning Styles* (Maidenhead, UK: Peter Honey, 1982).

2   John Dewey, *Experience and Education* (New York: Simon & Schuster, 1938), 20.

3   David A. Kolb, *Experiential Learning: Experience as the Source of Learning and Development* (Upper Saddle River, NJ: Prentice Hall, 1984), 41.

4   Preben Vang and Terry Carter, *Telling God's Story: The Biblical Narrative from Beginning to End* (Nashville: Broadman & Holman, 2006), 9.

5   Maryellen Weirmer, *Learner-Centered Teaching: Five Key Changes to Practice* (San Francisco: Jossey-Bass, 2002).

CHAPTER TEN

1   "Chronological Bible Storying: Introduction," Orality Strategies, accessed July, 11. 2013, https://www.oralitystrategies.org/strategies.cfm?id=1.

CHAPTER ELEVEN

1   Erika A Patall, Harris Cooper, Susuan R. Wynn, "The Effectiveness and Relative Importance of Choice in the Classroom", *Journal of Educational Psychology,* vol. 102, no. 4, November 2010: 896–915, http://psycnet.apa.org/psycarticles/2010-19093-001.

2   Henryk Skolimowski, *The Theatre of the Mind: Evolution in the Sensitive Cosmos* (Wheaton, IL: Theosophical Publishing House, 1984), 25.

3   Terry Doyle, *Helping Students Learn in a Learner-centered Environment* (Sterling, VA: Stylus Publishing, 2008), 45.

4   Arthur, *The God-Hungry Imagination*, 149.

ENDNOTES

CHAPTER TWELVE

1   Andy Root, *Unpacking Scripture in Youth Ministry* (Grand Rapids, MI: Zondervan: 2012), Chapter 2, Ebook Edition.

2   Joseph Lowman, *Mastering the Techniques of Teaching*, 2nd ed. (San Francisco: Jossey-Bass, 1995).

3   Henri J.M. Nouwen, *Bread for the Journey* (San Francisco: Harper Collins, 1997), 11.

4   Karen Lee-Thorp, *How to Ask Great Questions: Guide Your Group to Discovery With These Proven Techniques* (Colorado Springs, CO: NavPress, 1998).

5   Grahame Knox, *Creative Bible Study Methods for Youth Leaders*, Insight, 2007, 10-11, http://insight.typepad.co.uk/bible_study_methods.pdf.

6   Doug Pagitt, *Preaching Re-Imagined: The Role of the Sermon in Communities of Faith* (Grand Rapids, MI: Zondervan, 2005), 40.

CHAPTER THIRTEEN

1   Shoemaker, *GodStories*, xxv.